McDougal Littell

MODERN WORLD HISTORY

PATTERNS OF INTERACTION

In-Depth Resources: Unit 2

Absolutism to Revolution, 1500–1900

 McDougal Littell
A DIVISION OF HOUGHTON MIFFLIN COMPANY

Acknowledgments

CHAPTER 5

Excerpt from *Louis XIV, King of France and of Navarre: Mémoires for the Instruction of the Dauphin*, translated and notes by Paul Sonnino. Copyright © 1970 by The Free Press. Reprinted with the permission of The Free Press, a Division of Simon & Schuster, Inc.

Excerpt from *Imperial Russia: A Sourcebook, 1700–1917*, edited by Basil Dmytryshyn (New York: Holt, Rinehart and Winston, 1967), pp. 14–16, 18–19, 21–22. Reprinted by permission of Basil Dmytryshyn.

Excerpt from *The Cat and the King* by Louis Auchincloss. Copyright © 1981 by Louis Auchincloss. Reprinted by permission of Houghton Mifflin Company. All rights reserved.

CHAPTER 6

Excerpt from *Discoveries and Opinions of Galileo* by Galileo Galilei, edited and translated by Stillman Drake. Copyright © 1957 by Stillman Drake. Used by permission of Doubleday, a division of Bantam Doubleday Dell Publishing Group, Inc.

"A Friendly Commissar," from *The Recantation of Galileo Galilei* by Eric Bentley. Published by Northwestern University Press. Copyright © 1987 by Eric Bentley. All rights reserved. Reprinted by permission of Northwestern University Press.

CHAPTER 7

The "Marseillaise," from *Words of Fire, Deeds of Blood* by Olivier Bernier. Translation Copyright © 1989 by Olivier Bernier. Reprinted by permission of Little, Brown and Company.

CHAPTER 8

Excerpt from *All Souls' Rising* by Madison Smartt Bell. Copyright © 1995 by Madison Smartt Bell. Reprinted by permission of Pantheon Books, a division of Random House, Inc.

The editors have made every effort to trace the ownership of all copyrighted selections found in this book and to make full acknowledgment for their use. Omissions brought to our attention will be corrected in a subsequent edition.

ISBN-13: 978-0-618-40976-1 ISBN-10: 0-618-40976-9

Printed in the United States of America.

5 6 7 8 9 - CKI - 09 08 07 06

Unit 2 Absolutism to Revolution 1500–1900

CHAPTER 5 Absolute Monarchs in Europe, 1500–1800

GUIDED READING
- Section 1 1
- Section 2 2
- Section 3 3
- Section 4 4
- Section 5 5

BUILDING VOCABULARY 6

SKILLBUILDER PRACTICE: Evaluating Decisions 7

GEOGRAPHY APPLICATION: Old Empires and New Powers 8

PRIMARY SOURCES
- Louis XIV's Advice to His Son 10
- Peter the Great's Reforms 11
- from the *Diary of Samuel Pepys* 12
- from the English Bill of Rights 13

LITERATURE SELECTION
- from *The Cat and the King* by Louis Auchincloss 14

HISTORYMAKERS
- Maria Theresa 17
- William of Orange 18

CONNECTIONS ACROSS TIME AND CULTURES
- The Absolute Power of Rulers 19

RETEACHING ACTIVITIES
- Section 1 20
- Section 2 21
- Section 3 22
- Section 4 23
- Section 5 24

CHAPTER 6 Enlightenment and Revolution, 1550–1789

GUIDED READING
- Section 1 25
- Section 2 26
- Section 3 27
- Section 4 28

BUILDING VOCABULARY 29

SKILLBUILDER PRACTICE: Clarifying 30

GEOGRAPHY APPLICATION: Three Theories of the Solar System 31

PRIMARY SOURCES
- from *Starry Messenger* by Galileo Galilei 33
- from *The Social Contract* by Jean-Jacques Rousseau 34
- from *Two Treatises on Government* by John Locke 35
- from *A Vindication of the Rights of Woman* by Mary Wollstonecraft 36
- from The Declaration of Independence 37

LITERATURE SELECTION

from *The Recantation of Galileo Galilei* by Eric Bentley. 38

HISTORYMAKERS

Nicolaus Copernicus 41

Baron de Montesquieu 42

CONNECTIONS ACROSS TIME AND CULTURES

The Search for Truth and Reason 43

RETEACHING ACTIVITIES

Section 1 44

Section 2 45

Section 3 46

Section 4 47

CHAPTER ⑦ The French Revolution and Napoleon, 1789–1815

GUIDED READING

Section 1 48

Section 2 49

Section 3 50

Section 4 51

Section 5 52

BUILDING VOCABULARY 53

SKILLBUILDER PRACTICE: Interpreting Maps 54

GEOGRAPHY APPLICATION: The French Revolution Under Siege 55

PRIMARY SOURCES

from A Declaration of the Rights of Man and of the Citizen. 57

La Marseillaise. 58

from The Execution of Louis XVI by Henry Essex Edgeworth de Firmont 59

Napoleon's Proclamation at Austerlitz 60

LITERATURE SELECTION

from *A Tale of Two Cities* by Charles Dickens. 61

HISTORYMAKERS

Marie Antoinette 64

Maximilien Robespierre. 65

CONNECTIONS ACROSS TIME AND CULTURES

Comparing Revolutions in America and France 66

SCIENCE & TECHNOLOGY

Science Helps Create the Metric System. 67

RETEACHING ACTIVITIES

Section 1 68

Section 2 69

Section 3 70

Section 4 71

Section 5 72

CHAPTER ⑧ Nationalist Revolutions Sweep the West, 1789–1900

GUIDED READING

Section 1 73

Section 2 74

Section 3 75

Section 4 76

BUILDING VOCABULARY 77

SKILLBUILDER PRACTICE: Hypothesizing 78

GEOGRAPHY APPLICATION: Languages Fuel Nationalism 79

PRIMARY SOURCES

from Proclamation of 1813 by Simón Bolívar 81

Letter to Thomas Moore from George Gordon, Lord Byron 82

Proclamation of 1860 by Giuseppe Garibaldi 83

Nationalist Speech by Otto von Bismarck 84

LITERATURE SELECTION

from *All Souls' Rising* by Madison Smartt Bell 85

HISTORYMAKERS

Simón Bolívar 88

Ludwig van Beethoven 89

CONNECTIONS ACROSS TIME AND CULTURES

Bonds That Create a Nation-State 90

RETEACHING ACTIVITIES

Section 1 91

Section 2 92

Section 3 93

Section 4 94

ANSWER KEY 95

Name _____ Date _____

GUIDED READING *Spain's Empire and European Absolutism*

A. *Analyzing Causes and Recognizing Effects* As you read about the Spanish Empire, briefly note the causes or effects (depending on which is missing) of each event or situation.

Causes	Effects
1. The gold and silver coming from its vast empire made Spain incredibly wealthy.	
2.	Spain suffered from severe inflation.
3.	The Spanish economy declined and at times Spain was bankrupt.
4. Philip raised taxes in the Netherlands and tried to crush Protestantism.	
5.	The Dutch became wealthy from trade and banking.
6.	European monarchs became increasingly more powerful.

B. *Determining Main Ideas* On the back of this paper, explain how **Philip II** was an example of an **absolute monarch**.

Name _____ Date _____

A. *Clarifying* As you read about the French monarchy, write notes to answer the questions.

Wars between the Huguenots and Catholics create chaos in France.	
1. How did Henry of Navarre end the crisis and restore order?	
2. How did Cardinal Richelieu strengthen the French monarchy?	
3. What effect did the religious wars have on French intellectuals?	

Louis XIV became the most powerful monarch of his time.	
4. What steps did Jean Baptiste Colbert take to turn France into an economic power?	
5. In what ways did Louis XIV support the arts?	
6. Why did Louis fail in his attempts to expand the French Empire?	
7. What was the legacy of Louis XIV?	

B. *Summarizing* On the back of this paper, define the terms **skepticism** and **intendant**.

Name _____ Date _____

GUIDED READING *Central European*
Monarchs Clash

A. *Clarifying* As you read about the absolute monarchs that ruled in Central Europe,
fill out the chart by writing notes in the appropriate spaces.

The Thirty Years' War	
1. Note two causes of the war.	
2. Note four consequences of the war and the Peace of Westphalia.	

Central Europe	
3. Note two differences between the economies of western and central Europe.	
4. Note two reasons why central European empires were weak.	

Prussia and Austria	
5. Note three steps the Hapsburgs took to become more powerful.	
6. Note three steps the Hohenzollerns took to build up their state.	

B. *Synthesizing* On the back of this paper, write a brief assessment of **Maria
Theresa** and **Frederick the Great** as rulers.

Name _____ Date _____

GUIDED READING *Absolute Rulers of Russia*

A. *Identifying Solutions* As you read this section, complete the chart by explaining how Peter the Great solved each problem he encountered in his efforts to westernize Russia.

Problems	Solutions
1. Russian people did not believe that change was necessary.	
2. The Russian Orthodox Church was too strong.	
3. The great landowners had too much power.	
4. The Russian army was untrained and its tactics and weapons were outdated.	
5. Russian society had to change to compete with the modern states of Europe.	
6. To promote education and growth, Russia needed a seaport for travel to the West.	
7. The port needed to be built.	
8. The new city needed to be settled.	

B. *Drawing Conclusions* On the back of this paper, write a paragraph to identify Ivan IV and explain why he is called **Ivan the Terrible.**

GUIDED READING   *Parliament Limits the*
English Monarchy

A. *Summarizing* As you read this section, take notes to fill in the diagram describing relations between Parliament and each English ruler listed.

1. King James I (1603–1625)

↓

2. Charles I (1625–1649)

↓

3. Oliver Cromwell (1649–1658)

↓

4. Charles II (1660–1685)

↓

5. James II (1685–1688)

↓

6. William and Mary (1689–1702)

B. *Clarifying* On the back of this paper define or identify each term below.

Restoration   **habeas corpus**   **Glorious Revolution**   **cabinet**   **constitutional monarch**

Name _____ Date _____

A. *Multiple Choice* Circle the letter before the term or name that best completes the sentence.

1. The Catholic king of Spain who launched the Spanish Armada in an attempt to punish Protestants in England was (a) Louis XIV (b) Philip II (c) Charles I.

2. The idea that nothing can ever be known for certain is called (a) skepticism (b) *habeas corpus* (c) westernization.

3. The real ruler of France during the reign of Louis XIII was (a) Jean Baptiste Colbert (b) Maria Teresa (c) Cardinal Richelieu.

4. The most powerful ruler in French history was (a) Frederick the Great (b) Louis XIV (c) Peter the Great.

5. The czar who promoted the westernization of Russia was (a) Ivan the Terrible (b) Frederick the Great (c) Peter the Great.

6. The conflict over religion, territory, and power among Europe's ruling families that resulted in the modern state system was the (a) War of the Spanish Succession (b) Thirty Years' War (c) Seven Years' War.

B. *Evaluating* Write *T* in the blank if the statement is true. If the statement is false, write *F* in the blank and then write the corrected statement on the line below.

_____ 1. Maria Teresa was the ruler of France and Frederick the Great was the ruler of Austria during the Seven Years' War, in which the great European powers fought one another on three continents.

_____

_____ 2. In the English Civil War, Charles I of England was defeated by a Puritan general named Oliver Cromwell.

_____

_____ 3. The rule of Charles II in England is known as the Glorious Revolution because the monarchy was brought back.

_____

C. *Writing* Write a paragraph explaining how England's form of government changed after 1688 using the following terms.

absolute monarch   divine right   constitutional monarchy

CHAPTER 5

Section 4

SKILLBUILDER PRACTICE *Evaluating Decisions*

Historians evaluate decisions made in the past on the basis of short- and long-term consequences as well as moral implications. As you have read, Peter the Great was determined to westernize Russia and the Russian people. The passage below describes the first decision Peter made upon his arrival home from Europe. Evaluate this decision by answering the questions that follow. (See Skillbuilder Handbook)

Surprisingly enough, the first thing Peter reformed when he returned to the Kremlin was not the army or industries but beards. To Peter, the Russian custom of wearing beards symbolized everything that was backward about his country. When his nobles fell on their knees to welcome him home, the czar raised them up, took out a long European razor, and commanded them to hold still while he shaved off their beards. The boyars were horrified. Russian men of the time treasured their beards as symbols of manhood and Christianity. The tradition of the Orthodox Church held that God had a beard and as man was made in God's image, he too must be bearded. Yet Peter decreed that all Russian nobles must shave off their beards. To make sure his decree was obeyed, he posted barbers at Moscow's gates. Noblemen who wished to keep their beards had to pay a beard tax every year and hang a metal tag from their necks to prove that they had indeed paid it. Without this tag, a man's beard could be clipped on sight.

Peter also issued an edict commanding that all boyars and members of the gentry class adopt western-style clothing. The manufacturing of traditional Russian dress, most commonly long cloaks with flowing sleeves, was made illegal. These edicts, although not of great significance, were regarded by many Russians as an attack on personal freedoms and valued traditions. Foreign ways were being forced on the Russian people against their will. This attack on traditional Russian garb began a debate in Russia—one that continues today—about whether to westernize Russia or to focus instead on traditional culture.

1. What were some short-term effects of Peter's decision to modernize the appearance

of Russian men? _____

_____

2. What were some long-term effects of that decision? _____

_____

3. One historian describes Peter's decision as "an action full of symbolism." In what way

was Peter's decision symbolic? _____

_____

4. How would you evaluate Peter's decision? Was the decision a good one or not?

Explain why you think as you do. _____

_____

_____

GEOGRAPHY APPLICATION: LOCATION
Old Empires and New Powers

Section 3

Directions: Read the paragraphs below and study the maps carefully. Then answer the questions that follow.

A period of political transition in central and eastern Europe followed the end of the Thirty Years' War, in 1648. The declining powers of Poland, the Holy Roman Empire, and the Ottoman Empire faced not only a deterioration of their influence, but outright extinction from Europe. Prussia, the Russian Empire, and the Austrian Empire emerged as powerful forces on the European continent.

The three declining powers shared many characteristics. In all of them, central power became weak. They lacked efficient systems of government and administration. In addition, the people in the these empires were difficult to govern because they consisted of many nationalities and spoke a variety of languages. Finally, none of the empires formed their people into a strong organization. As a result, the Polish Republic ceased to exist in 1795, while the Holy Roman Empire disappeared in 1806.

However, the Ottoman Empire, though crumbling and weak, managed to maintain itself until 1922.

The 17th century saw the emergence of a new kind of national state. These new states were built on a strong monarch, a standing army, and a professional civil service and administration. These new powers sought to fill the "political vacuum" created in central Europe by the declining empires. Leaderless populations could easily be shifted inside the political boundaries by the monarchs of newer national states. As a result, these new powers led by the Hohenzollerns of Prussia, the Romanovs of Russia, and the Hapsburgs of Austria formed or expanded their states in the void created by the "soft" rule of these aging empires.

These three new empires, in turn, would influence the course of European history for the next 200 years.

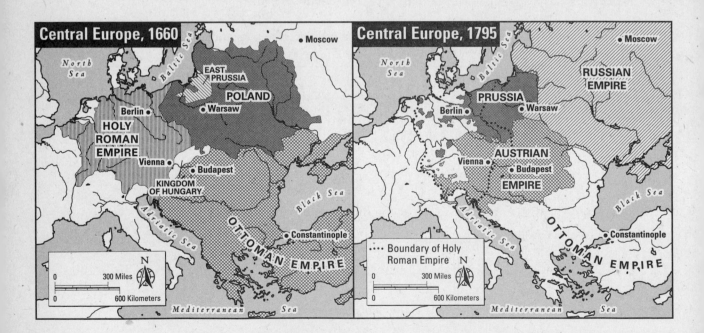

Interpreting Text and Visuals

1. What new power swallows the Kingdom of Hungary? _____

_____

2. What empires are shown on both maps? Which increase? Which decrease? _____

_____

3. By 1795, the lands of Poland were divided up by what other empires? _____

_____

4. Examine again the location of the Ottoman Empire. Why do you think it was able to last the

   longest out of the three aging powers? _____

_____

_____

_____

5. How many miles separate Moscow and the Russian border in 1660? 1795? _____

_____

6. What problems caused the decline of Poland, the Holy Roman Empire, and the Ottoman Empire?

_____

_____

_____

_____

7. Describe the characteristics that enabled Russia, Austria, and Prussia to rise to power. _____

_____

_____

_____

CHAPTER
5

Section 2

PRIMARY SOURCE Louis XIV's Advice to His Son

When he was in his twenties, Louis XIV began writing down his thoughts about being a ruler. His Mémoires for the Instruction of the Dauphin *illuminated how he became the strongest king of his time. In this excerpt from his book, Louis XIV shares his recipe for absolute rule with his son. What steps did he take to consolidate his power after the death of Mazarin?*

I commanded the four secretaries of state not to sign anything at all any longer without discussing it with me, the superintendant likewise, and for nothing to be transacted at the finances without being registered in a little book that was to remain with me, where I could always see at a glance, briefly summarized, the current balance and the expenditures made or pending.

The Chancellor received a similar order, that is, not to seal anything without my command, except for letters of justice. . . .

I announced that all requests for graces of any type had to be made directly to me, and I granted to all my subjects without distinction the privilege of appealing to me at any time, in person or by petitions. The petitions were initially very numerous, which did not discourage me, however. The disorder into which my affairs had fallen produced many of them, the idle or unjustified hopes which were raised by this novelty hardly stimulated a lesser number. . . . But even in these apparently useless things I discovered much that was useful. I learned thereby many details about the condition of my people. They saw that I was concerned about them, and nothing did so much to win me their hearts. . . .

As to the persons who were to support me in my work, I resolved above all not to have a prime minister, and if you and all your successors take my advice, my son, the name will forever be abolished in France, there being nothing more shameful than to see on the one hand all the functions and on the other the mere title of king.

For this purpose, it was absolutely necessary to divide my confidence and the execution of my orders without entirely entrusting it to anyone, assigning these various persons to various functions in keeping with their various talents, which is perhaps the first and foremost talent of princes.

In order to concentrate the entire authority of a master more fully in myself—even though there are all sorts of details into which our occupations and our very dignity do not usually permit us to go, I resolved to enter into these with each of the ministers whom I would choose, and when he would least expect it, so that he would realize that I might do the same on other subjects and at any time. . . .

It is not so easy for me to tell you, my son, how to go about the choice of the various ministers. Fortune always plays, in spite of us, at least as much of a part in it as wisdom; and in the part that wisdom plays, intelligence can do far more than counsel. Neither of us, my son, is going to seek for these sorts of positions those whom distance and obscurity remove from our view, whatever qualifications they may have. It is necessary to decide from a small number which chance presents to us, that is, those already in office or whom birth and inclination have attached to our personal service.

And as for this art of knowing men, which will be so important to you not merely on this but also on every other occasion of your life, I shall tell you, my son, that it can be learned but that it can not be taught.

from Paul Sonnino, trans., *Louis XIV: Mémoires for the Instruction of the Dauphin* (New York: The Free Press, 1970), 30–32.

Activity Options

1. *Recognizing Point of View* With a partner, role-play a conversation between Louis XIV and his son in which the king advises how to rule absolutely.
2. *Writing for a Specific Purpose* List the steps that Louis XIV took to consolidate his power as king of France after the death of Cardinal Mazarin. Then share your list with classmates and compare Louis XIV's approach to governing with that of his father, Louis XIII.

CHAPTER
5
Section 4

PRIMARY SOURCE Peter the Great's Reforms

Czar Peter I of Russia, known as Peter the Great, visited western Europe in 1697 to learn more about European customs and industry. Inspired by his trip, he sought to westernize Russia in order to strengthen Russia's position in the modern world. How did the following decrees change daily life in Russia?

A Decree on a New Calendar

The Great Sovereign has ordered it declared: the Great Sovereign knows that many European Christian countries as well as Slavic peoples are in complete accord with our Eastern Orthodox Church . . . —all these peoples number their years from eight days after the birth of Christ, this is from January 1, and not from the creation of the world. There is a great difference in those two calendars. This year is 1699 since the birth of Christ, and on January 1 it will be 1700 as well as a new century. To celebrate this happy and opportune occasion, the Great Sovereign has ordered that henceforth all government administrative departments and fortresses in all their official business use the new calendar beginning January 1, 1700. To commemorate this happy beginning and the new century in the capital city of Moscow, after a solemn prayer in churches and private dwellings, all major streets, homes of important people, and homes of distinguished religious and civil servants should be decorated with trees, pine, and fir branches similar to the decoration of the Merchant Palace or the Pharmacy Building—or as best as one knows how to decorate his place and gates. Poor people should put up at least one tree, or a branch on their gates or on their apartment [doors]. These decorations are to remain from January 1 to January 7, 1700. As a sign of happiness on January 1, friends should greet each other and the New Year and the new century as follows: when the Red Square will be lighted and shooting will begin—followed by that at the homes of boyars, courtiers, and important officials of the tsar, military and merchant classes—everyone who has a musket or any other fire arm should either salute thrice or shoot several rockets or as many as he has. . . .

Decrees on Compulsory Education of the Russian Nobility

Send to every gubernia [region] some persons from mathematical schools to teach the children of the nobility—except those of freeholders and gov-

ernment clerks—mathematics and geometry; as a penalty [for evasion] establish a rule that no one will be allowed to marry unless he learns these [subjects]. Inform all prelates to issue no marriage certificates to those who are ordered to go to schools. . . .

The Great Sovereign has decreed: in all gubernias children between the ages of ten and fifteen of the nobility, of government clerks, and of lesser officials, except those of freeholders, must be taught mathematics and some geometry. Toward that end, students should be sent from mathematical schools [as teachers], several into each gubernia, to prelates and to renowned monasteries to establish schools. During their instruction these teachers should be given food and financial remuneration . . . from gubernia revenues set aside for that purpose by personal orders of His Imperial Majesty. No fees should be collected from students. When they have mastered the material, they should then be given certificates written in their own handwriting. When the students are released they ought to pay one ruble each for their training. Without these certificates they should not be allowed to marry nor receive marriage certificates.

from Basil Dmytryshyn, *Imperial Russia: A Sourcebook, 1700–1917* (New York: Holt, Rinehart and Winston, Inc., 1967), 14–22. Reprinted in Peter N. Stearns, ed., *Documents in World History,* Vol. II (New York: Harper Collins Publishers, 1988), 32–34.

Discussion Questions
Clarifying
1. When did the new Russian calendar go into effect and how did Russia celebrate?
2. What penalty did children of Russian nobles face if they did not learn mathematics?
3. **Drawing Conclusions** What advantages do you think Russia gained by these reforms? What disadvantages, if any, do you see?

CHAPTER 5

Section 5

PRIMARY SOURCE *from the* Diary *of* Samuel Pepys

On September 2, 1666, the worst fire in London's history broke out in the house of the king's baker near London Bridge. Samuel Pepys (1633–1703), an English civil servant, recorded his firsthand impressions of the fire in his diary. As you read this entry, keep in mind that Pepys uses 17th-century English spellings, sentence structure, and capitalization.

September 2 1666 Lords day. Some of our maids sitting up late last night to get things ready against our feast today, Jane called us up, about 3 in the morning, to tell us of a great fire they saw in the City. So I rose, and slipped on my nightgown and went to her window, and thought it to be on the back side of Markelane at the furthest; but being unused to such fires as fallowed, I thought it far enough off, and so went to bed again and to sleep. About 7 rose again to dress myself, and there looked out at the window and saw the fire not so much as it was, and further off. So to my closet to set things to rights after yesterday's cleaning. By and by Jane comes and tells me that she hears that above 300 houses have been burned down tonight by the fire we saw, and that it was now burning down all Fishstreet by London Bridge. So I made myself ready presently, and walked to the Tower and there got up upon one of the high places, Sir J. Robinsons little son going up with me; and there I did see the houses at that end of the bridge all on fire, and an infinite great fire on this and the other side the end of the bridge—which, among other people, did trouble me for poor little Michell and our Sarah on the Bridge. So down, with my heart full of trouble, to the Lieutenant of the Tower, who tells me that it begun this morning in the King's bakers house in Pudding-lane, and that it hath burned down St Magnes Church and most part of Fishstreete already. So I down to the water-side and there got a boat and through bridge, and there saw a lamentable fire. Poor Michells house, as far as the Old Swan, already burned that way and the fire running further, that in a very little time it got as far as the Stillyard while I was there. Everybody endeavouring to remove their goods, and flinging into the River or bringing them into lighters [large flat-bottomed barges] that lay off. Poor people staying in their houses as long as till the very fire touched them, and then running into boats or clambering from one pair of stair by the water-side

to another. And among other things, the poor pigeons I perceive were loath to leave their houses, but hovered about the windows and balconies till they were some of them burned, their wings, and fell down. . . .

. . . So near the fire as we could for smoke; and all over the Thames, with one's face in the wind you were almost burned with a shower of Firedrops—this is very true—so as houses were burned by these drops and flakes of fire, three or four, nay five or six houses, one from another. When we could endure no more upon the water, we to a little alehouse on the Bankside over against the Three Cranes, and there stayed till it was dark almost and saw the fire grow; and as it grow darker, appeared more and more, and in Corners and upon steeples and between churches and houses, as far as we could see up the hill of the City, in a most horrid malicious bloody flame, not like a fine flame of an ordinary fire. Barbary and her husband away before us. We stayed till, it being darkish, we saw the fire as only one entire arch of fire from this to the other side of the bridge, and in a bow up the hill, for an arch of above a mile long. It made me weep to see it. The churches, houses, and all on fire and flaming at once, and a horrid noise the flames made, and the cracking of houses at their ruine.

from Robert Latham and William Matthews, eds., *Diary of Samuel Pepys* (G. Bell & Sons, 1970–83). Reprinted in John Carey, ed., *Eyewitness to History* (New York: Avon Books, 1987), 188–191.

Activity Options

1. *Analyzing Causes and Recognizing Effects* Working with a partner, create a cause-and-effect chart to illustrate the effects of the London fire according to Pepys.
2. *Writing for a Specific Purpose* Write a lead paragraph for a newspaper report of what happened in London on September 2, 1666. Share your paragraph with the class.

CHAPTER 5

Section 5

PRIMARY SOURCE *from the* English Bill of Rights

After the Glorious Revolution in 1688 in which James II was overthrown, England's absolute monarchy became a constitutional monarchy where laws limited royal power. In 1689, Parliament drafted a Bill of Rights, stating the rights of Parliament and of individuals. As you read a portion of the English Bill of Rights, think about what England's monarchs could not do.

The English Bill of Rights, 1689

Whereas the said late King James II having abdicated the government, and the throne being thereby vacant, his Highness the prince of Orange (whom it hath pleased Almighty God to make the glorious instrument of delivering this kingdom from popery and arbitrary power) did (by the advice of the lords spiritual and temporal, and diverse principal persons of the Commons) caused letters to be written to the lords spiritual and temporal, being Protestants . . . to meet and sit at Westminster upon the two and twentieth day of January, in this year 1689, in order to such an establishment as that their religion, laws, and liberties might not again be in danger of being subverted; upon which letters elections have been accordingly made.

And thereupon the said lords spiritual and temporal and Commons, pursuant to their respective letters and elections, being now assembled in a full and free representation of this nation, taking into their most serious consideration the best means for attaining the ends aforesaid, do in the first place (as their ancestors in like case have usually done), for the vindication and assertion of their ancient rights and liberties, declare:

1. That the pretended power of suspending laws, or the execution of laws, by regal authority, without consent of parliament is illegal.
2. That the pretended power of dispensing with the laws, or the execution of law by regal authority, as it hath been assumed and exercised of late, is illegal.
3. That the commission for erecting the late court of commissioners for ecclesiastical [religious] causes, and all other commissions and courts of like nature, are illegal and pernicious [destructive].
4. That levying money for or to the use of the crown by pretense of prerogative, without grant of parliament, for longer time or in other manner than the same is or shall be granted, is illegal.
5. That it is the right of the subjects to petition the king, and all commitments and prosecutions for such petitioning are illegal.
6. That the raising or keeping a standing army within the kingdom in time of peace, unless it be with consent of parliament, is against law.
7. That the subjects which are Protestants may have arms for their defense suitable to their conditions, and as allowed by law.
8. That election of members of parliament ought to be free.
9. That the freedom of speech, and debates or proceedings in parliament, ought not to be impeached or questioned in any court or place out of parliament.
10. That excessive bail ought not to be required, nor excessive fines imposed, nor cruel and unusual punishments inflicted. . . .
13. And that for redress of all grievance and for the amending, strengthening, and preserving of the laws, parliament ought to be held frequently. And they do claim, demand, and insist upon all and singular the premises, as their undoubted rights and liberties. . . .

from E. P. Cheyney, *Readings in English History* (New York: Ginn and Company, 1922), 545–547. Reprinted in Peter N. Stearns, ed., *Documents in World History*, Vol. II (New York: Harper Collins Publishers, 1988), 13–14.

Research Option

Comparing and Contrasting Read the United States Constitution's Bill of Rights. Then make a Venn diagram in which you compare and contrast the American Bill of Rights and the English Bill of Rights. Share your diagram with a small group of classmates.

CHAPTER

5

Section 2

LITERATURE SELECTION *from* **The Cat and the King**
by Louis Auchincloss

The Cat and the King is a work of historical fiction about Louis XIV. The novel's narrator—Louis de Rouvroy, the second duc de Saint-Simon—is based on a real-life French noble who observed life at the court of Louis XIV and recorded in his memoirs all that he saw and felt about the reign of the Sun King. The following excerpt, which is drawn from an incident that actually happened, takes place shortly after Saint-Simon has married Gabrielle. What impressions of Louis XIV and life at Versailles does this passage convey?

Gabrielle's first substantial contribution to my career at court was in the affair of the alms bag. It was the custom after mass for the young duchesse de Bourgogne, the king's grand-daughter-in-law, who, as we had lost both queen and dauphine, was the first lady of France, to ask a duchess to pass a velvet purse for contributions to the church. The "Lorrainers," members of the House of Guise, who should have ranked with us as peers, were always claiming a higher position as "foreign princes," based on silly titles bestowed on them by the Holy Roman Emperor because of scraps of land held along the border. I now learned the latest outrage: that their ladies were claiming exemption from the almsbag duty. There was nothing for me to do but organize the dukes to make a similar claim.

"But who will pass the alms bag?" Gabrielle asked me.

"How should I know? Perhaps some simple gentlewoman."

"But if the duchess asks me?"

"If she asks you, of course, you must. But she can't ask you if you're not there. What I'm saying is that the duchesses should abstain from mass."

"Won't it anger the king?"

"I can't help that, my dear. It's the Lorrainers he should be mad at. They've been an infernal nuisance ever since the days of the League. Why a monarch who's so sensitive to treason should put up with them, I can't conceive."

Gabrielle, I had to admit, was correct about the king's reaction. After the first day, when half the duchesses at court absented themselves from mass, the duc de Beauvillier sent for me, and Gabrielle and I went at once to his apartment in the north wing. The duke, who, as I have indicated, was the only peer in the king's council, was an old friend of my parents and had been my guide and mentor ever since I first came to court. I admired him without reserve and had even once offered to marry any one of his eight daughters. Fortunately for me and Gabrielle, the oldest had wished to take holy orders, the second had been a cripple and the rest too young.

"I think you ought to know," Beauvillier told me, "that the king spoke of you this morning at the end of the council. He said that ever since you had resigned your commission, you have been obsessed with petty questions of rank and precedence."

"Oh, he remembered about my commission?" I had left the army, two years before, to devote myself to the court.

"The king remembers everything."

"Then I wish he would remember the countless disloyalties of the Lorrainers!"

"If he doesn't appear to, you can be sure he has a reason. In any case, he wishes me to convey to you his desire that the duchesse de Saint-Simon should pass the alms bag on Monday."

I hesitated. "Is that an order, sir?"

"Is the king's desire not always an order?"

"Very well. But surely I need not be present. He will not require me to assist at my own humiliation?"

"That is up to you."

"Ah, but, my dear, may I make a suggestion?"

I turned to Gabrielle in mild surprise. It was not like her to intervene in my conversation with an older person. "Certainly."

"Request an audience with the king! Tell him you raised the issue of the alms bag only because you thought it was one in which he was not concerned. But now that you know he wants me to carry the bag, you are not only proud but honored!"

I looked into her anxious eyes with even greater surprise. Then I turned to the old duke.

"Do it, Saint-Simon!" he exclaimed with a laugh. "And be thankful for a smart little wife."

"And then ask the king for an apartment in the palace!" Gabrielle hurriedly added.

"Speak to him at his dinner," Beauvillier advised me. "Request an audience for tomorrow. I'll put in a word for you at the coucher [bed time]." He glanced at his watch. "It's almost one now. Hurry up if you want a spot near his table!"

The king liked to sup with members of his family, but he was inclined to dine alone, that is, alone at table. There was always a group of courtiers standing by the small table at which he was served, silently regarding him. He ate, as he did everything else, with remarkable solemnity, dignity and grace. He would rise a chicken bone to his lips, take an incisive, effective bite and then chew slowly, his dark, glazed eyes focused in an opaque stare. When he turned his head to survey the room or the watching crowd, this stare might be softened to encompass not an acknowledgment, certainly not a greeting, but simply a recognition. Somehow you always knew that he knew you. And he not only knew who was present; he knew who was not.

There was something hypnotic about the effect of one man exercising a natural function while his audience remained motionless. It was like watching a priest take communion. The huge, high-piled black perruque [wig] moved rhythmically with the royal mastications; the high, arched brows twitched; the great aquiline nose snorted after the thick lips had sipped wine. His most ordinary acts were majestical. . . .

It was permissible for those standing closest to the table to address the king when he was not actually swallowing or masticating. Waiting until his gaze took me in, I stepped forward and bowed.

"May I be permitted a word, sire, on the question of the alms bag?"

The dark eyes emitted a faint glitter. "There is no question, sir. The matter has been regulated."

"But, sire, I humbly suggest there has been a misapprehension of my attitude. I wish only to make explicit my utter loyalty and devotion."

"Very well, then. When you wish."

> *The huge, high-piled black perruque [wig] moved rhythmically with the royal mastications; the high, arched brows twitched; the great aquiline nose snorted after the thick lips had sipped wine.*

He turned to his goblet, and I stepped quickly back. So far, so good. After dinner Beauvillier told me exactly what to do next. I should stand in the front row of the courtiers waiting outside the council chamber the following morning and step immediately forward when the king came out. He would then appoint a time for an audience, perhaps immediately. It was all simple enough, but nonetheless I hardly closed my eyes that night, and Gabrielle made me drink two glasses of wine with breakfast.

At noon, outside the council chamber, I did as I had been told. The king paused to give me one of his glacial stares, a mixture of surprise and faint irritation. Then he must have recollected what Beauvillier had told him at the coucher, for, beckoning me to follow him, he stepped into the embrasure [opening in a thick wall] of a window, where he folded his arms and waited for me to speak.

I began with what I had intended to be the very briefest summary of the alms-bag controversy, but he interrupted me testily.

"I have no time, sir, for such nit-picking. You spend your life fussing over imagined slights. You had far better have stayed in the army, where you were of some use."

I saw at once that the situation was desperate. I even dared now to raise my voice.

"I had no intention, sire, of bringing up the issue of ducal rights. I only wish to tell you that, as a duke, my sole aim is to be of service to you. Had the duchesse de Saint-Simon and I known in the beginning that it was your desire that she should pass the alms bag, she would have passed it joyfully, and with my total blessing, among the humblest in the land, in the most fetid of hospitals, in the darkest of dungeons!"

The king's countenance at last relaxed. "Now that's talking," he said in a milder tone.

I went on, carried away by my excitement, to declaim on my loyalty and that of my ancestors; to tell him that we were second to none in our zeal for the royal service. The king let me continue in this way for what must have been several minutes before interrupting me at last by raising his hand.

And then, to my astonishment, it was to answer me in a tone that was almost benign!

At first, I hardly took in what he was saying. His effect on me was hypnotic. I kept my gaze so firmly fixed upon his lips, not presuming to look him in the eye, that soon I began to feel a bit dizzy. His opening and closing orifice conjured up in my fantasy the mouth of a cave in the middle of a desert of infinite range and emptiness. It was as if no life could be contained in the parching dryness; that only in the darkness behind that agitated adit [entrance to a mine] could there exist sustenance and support. But how could one make the passage past those teeth with any hope of safety? I was hearing the king, a voice kept saying to me! I was actually hearing the king!

And then the purport of his words began again to come through to me. His tone was almost avuncular [like an uncle].

"I had not thought, sir, that you had a proper excuse for quitting the army. However, if you truly wish to be of service here at court, there will always be occasion. But let me give a piece of advice. You must watch that tongue of yours! It is too inclined to be free. If you take care of that, I shall take care of you. I do not forget that my father loved yours."

This reference to my beloved progenitor completely undid me. The tears, I am not ashamed to admit, started to my eyes, and I proceeded to pour forth my gratitude. I do not recall everything I said, but I know that I must have expressed with passion my desire to serve him in all matters. I ended by begging to be considered for any rooms in the château that might be available so that I should have more ample opportunity to pay my court. The reader, in another era, may smile, but he will not be able to imagine the effect of Louis XIV on his subjects when he chose to be gracious.

He spoke again. "I shall keep your request in mind." That measured tone always convinced the petitioner that his plea had been securely filed. "One never knows when a vacancy may occur."

And then, with that brief though definite, courteous though irrevocable nod, he moved on to the great gallery. I could feel in the very air of the chamber around me the soaring of my reputation.

Gabrielle met me in the antechamber with the round window known as the Oeil de Boeuf and took in at a glance the success of my audience. When she heard about the apartment, she clapped her hands.

"That means we're sure to get one!"

Indeed, she was right, for we were granted an apartment of three tiny rooms the very next day. They were hardly comfortable, yet they were more coveted than the greatest mansion. For only by living *in* Versailles could one fully appreciate the delights of the court. The palace at night had its peculiar pleasures and opportunities. The public was evicted, and the royal family retired behind closed doors, guarded by sleepy Swiss sentries. Something almost like informality prevailed.

It was a time for small, intimate suppers or conversations, for passionate post mortems of the day's events: who was in, who out, who had said what to Madame de Maintenon [Louis XIV's wife], who had been alone with the king. It was a time to call on the ministers and perhaps catch them, relaxed, in indiscretions. Oh, yes, an apartment was a great boon, and I was properly grateful to my wife.

"Now you've got everything you need!" she exclaimed proudly when we at last surveyed our redecorated reception chamber. I had even hung my father's portrait of the beloved Louis XIII over the little marble mantel.

"Need for what?"

"For whatever you want."

"And what do I want?"

"Ah, my dear, *you* must provide the answer to that!"

Discussion Questions

Clarifying

1. Who was involved in the so-called affair of the alms bag?
2. What was the outcome of Saint-Simon's audience with Louis XIV?
3. **Making Inferences** Based on your reading of this excerpt, how would you characterize the king's relationship with nobles such as Saint-Simon?

Name _____ Date _____

HISTORYMAKERS Maria Theresa
Dutiful Defender of Austria

". . . She could fight like a tiger and was at war for a large part of her reign; but she never fought [to gain land but] always . . . to preserve her inheritance. . . . She was not a zealously reforming queen. Her reforms were radical and far-reaching, but she reformed, as she fought, because she saw what had to be done. . . ."—Historian Edward Crankshaw on Maria Theresa

The 18th century was a time in which kings wrote the history of Europe. However, Maria Theresa of Austria emerged as a strong and powerful queen. She bravely defended Austria during a Prussian invasion and launched a series of domestic improvements that helped her people.

With no male heir, King Charles VI of Austria feared that other powers in Europe would try to seize his kingdom after his death. As a result, he convinced these European monarchs to accept Maria Theresa, his eldest daughter, as the next ruler of Austria. In 1740, Charles died, and the 23-year-old queen inherited a troubled country. Her people were uneasy. They thought that her husband would rule the nation, and they did not trust him. In addition, poor weather had produced bad harvests, and there was widespread hunger.

Maria Theresa learned about these worries by sending one of her ladies-in-waiting in disguise into Vienna to hear what her subjects were saying. For example, the people resented the fact that wild animals roamed the forests owned by the monarchy, eating food that they could eat. She won their approval by ordering the animals killed.

Just months after Maria Theresa became queen, Frederick II of Prussia moved his army into Silesia, Austria's richest region. Later in life, she wrote that she faced this situation ". . . without money, without credit, without an army, without experience and knowledge, even without counsel." Her father's old advisers gave her simple advice: give up Silesia.

The young queen proved to be made of sterner stuff. In June 1741, Maria Theresa received another of her titles, becoming the queen of Hungary. She then asked the Hungarian people for troops in her conflict with Prussia. "The very existence of the kingdom of Hungary, of our person, of our children, and our crown, are now at stake. . . ." she said. The war with Prussia dragged on for many years, and in the end Austria was forced to give up Silesia. Her stand had made a mark, however. All of

Europe now saw her diplomatic skill and her resolve to maintain her kingdom.

In 1756, the Seven Years' War began. This was Austria's attempt to win back Silesia. Maria Theresa had felt abandoned by Britain, an old ally of Austria, in that first war. She now formed a new alliance with Britain's longtime enemy, France. Britain, though, joined Prussia, and they won the war. However, Austria did not suffer additional loss of land.

For most of Maria Theresa's rule, she focused on improving conditions in her realm. She reformed the government, cutting the power of local authority and giving the Crown more control. She formed new schools to train people to serve in her government. She also won the right to set taxes for ten years at a time—in the past, local government bodies had set new levels of taxation each year. Now, she could count on a steady supply of money. Furthermore, the queen recognized that the peasants paid the major share of taxes in her kingdom. As a result, she issued laws that made that system fairer and limited the power of large landowners.

The queen also made the army larger and better trained. In addition, she issued an order to set up a public school system in Austrian lands. Finally, she brought people to settle rural areas where no one lived, which resulted in increased farmland.

Maria Theresa made these changes to strengthen her position, but they also benefited her people. Crankshaw summarizes her rule: "She had held her society together, encouraged its individual talents, and left it better than it was before."

Questions

1. ***Determining Main Ideas*** What would you say was the main idea of this biography?
2. ***Making Inferences*** How would you describe Maria Theresa's character?
3. ***Drawing Conclusions*** Would you say that Maria Theresa was a good queen? Explain.

HISTORYMAKERS William of Orange
Protestant Champion

"The Liberties of England and the Protestant Religion"—motto on the banners of William of Orange when he landed in England (1688)

William of Orange belonged to the royal families of two of the main Protestant powers in 17th century Europe—the Netherlands and England. As a result, he devoted himself to preventing the growth of Catholic France. It was to further that goal that he gladly accepted the offer to become king of England in 1688.

William was born to the house of Orange, a family that had helped the Netherlands win independence in the 1500s. In 1672, France and England invaded this country and William, though only 22 years old, was put in command of its army. The Dutch military had long been neglected, and parts of the country were quickly overrun. In desperation, William ordered the destruction of the dikes, devices that prevented the sea from flowing onto land. By flooding parts of his country, he prevented the advance of the enemy armies.

William then boldly refused a peace offer from England and France. Determined to continue the fight, William worked on two fronts. He strengthened the army while using diplomatic skill to find allies. He won some victories and within a few years forced the French to retreat.

During this time, William married his cousin, Mary. Both were grandchildren of King Charles I of England, and both had a claim to the English throne.

Throughout the early 1680s, William continued his efforts to limit French power. He wanted to ensure the survival of the Netherlands and prevent French religious influence. France was a Catholic nation, and William was the leading Protestant power in Europe. He had hoped to forge an alliance between the Netherlands and England, but the English never agreed to one.

In 1685, James, Mary's father and a Catholic, became king of England. That change brought William new opportunities. English Protestants feared that James would make the country Catholic again. They thought they could use William as a way to stop James. Some hoped that James would remain childless and that William and Mary would produce a son. Their child could be named to follow James on the throne to ensure that England

would remain Protestant. Others talked about naming William as a regent to control James. William, who was still seeking an alliance against France, listened to their plans.

In 1688, however, James and his wife had a son, a Catholic heir. A group of Protestant leaders then invited William to come to England and become king immediately. Skillfully avoiding James's strong navy, William crossed the English Channel. He landed with an army of 15,000, declared that a new Parliament should be elected, and easily marched to London. James fled for Europe.

Even then, William and Mary's status was uncertain. Some said that Mary should rule and that William, who was foreign born, should not have any real power. Nevertheless, Mary insisted that they rule together, and they were crowned king and queen. However, Mary died only a few years later.

William ruled both England and the Netherlands until 1702. He spent much of these years leading armies. First, he had to end revolts in Scotland and Ireland. Later, he fought on the continent, continuing his long struggle against France. He had a new cause for war now because Louis XIV of France was trying to put James back on the English throne. In early 1702, William urged Parliament to form an alliance with the Netherlands against France. While the bill was being debated, William died. Nevertheless, Parliament approved his plan and declared war on France. Parliament added that for the war to end, France must recognize the Protestant succession in England.

Questions

1. *Drawing Conclusions* Which of the ideas on William's banner do you think was more important to him? Why?
2. *Analyzing Causes and Recognizing Effects* Why did the English turn to William in the struggle with James?
3. *Synthesizing* What does *succession* mean and why was it important in England in this period?

Name _____ Date _____

CONNECTIONS ACROSS TIME AND CULTURES

The Absolute Power of Rulers

The theory of absolutism was not new to 16th century Europe. As far back as ancient river valley civilizations, kings had exerted complete control over their peoples' lives. How were European absolute monarchs similar to earlier ones? To find out, answer the questions that follow.

1. In Mesopotamia, kings were representatives of the gods. In Egypt, kings were gods. In ancient China, Zhou leaders introduced a concept of authority known as the **Mandate of Heaven.** According to this, a just ruler received his authority to rule from heaven; a king who was wicked or foolish lost the mandate and the right to rule. How did monarchs in Europe justify their right to rule? _____

_____

2. Absolute monarchs solidified their power in different ways. In Persia, King Darius appointed local governors called satraps to rule each province and then sent out inspectors throughout the kingdom to check on their loyalty. How did European rulers centralize power and control the nobility? _____

_____

3. Roman and Byzantine emperors controlled not just the state but the Church as well. How would you characterize relations between absolute monarchs in Europe and the Church? _____

_____

4. From the beginning of civilization, rulers have embarked on massive public works projects, often at the expense of human freedoms. Frequently, peasants had no choice but to work or die. How did European monarchs view human resources within their empires? _____

_____

5. In addition to building grand palaces, in what other ways did absolute rulers use the vast wealth they accumulated? _____

_____

6. What are some social, political, and economic conditions in a nation or empire that may lead to absolutism? _____

_____

CHAPTER
5
Section 1

RETEACHING ACTIVITY   *Spain's Empire and*
European Absolutism

Making Inferences Below are some general statements about Philip II's rule in
Spain. Read each statement. Then supply details from the section to support it.

1. Charles V, the Hapsburg king, was the first ruler after Charlemagne to control so much territory and hold so much power.

   a. _____

   b. _____

2. Philip II was an aggressive ruler for the Spanish empire.

   a. _____

   b. _____

3. Philip believed it was his duty to defend the Catholicism of the Spanish empire against the Muslims of the Ottoman Empire and the Protestants of Europe.

   a. _____

   b. _____

4. Spain experienced a golden age in the arts during the 16th and 17th centuries.

   a. _____

   b. _____

5. The materialism of the age brought Spain economic problems.

   a. _____

   b. _____

6. Spain's guilds played a role in its economic problems.

   a. _____

   b. _____

7. The Dutch part of the Spanish empire experienced prosperity while Spain struggled.

   a. _____

   b. _____

CHAPTER 5
Section 2

RETEACHING ACTIVITY *The Reign of Louis XIV*

Reading Comprehension Find the name or term in the second column that best matches the description in the first column. Then write the letter of your answer in the blank.

_____ 1. First king of the Bourbon dynasty in France

_____ 2. Declaration of religious toleration that allowed Huguenots to live in peace in France

_____ 3. Minister under Louis XIII who got France involved in the Thirty Years' War

_____ 4. Belief that nothing can be known for certain that caused some French thinkers to question the Church

_____ 5. Most powerful ruler in French history who weakened the power of the nobility

_____ 6. Government agents who collected taxes and administered justice under Louis XIV

_____ 7. Minister of finance under Louis XIV who strengthened French commerce

_____ 8. Splendid palace in which Louis XIV reigned

_____ 9. Writer of French comedies, one of which mocked religious hypocrisy

_____ 10. Struggle that ensued when England, Austria, the Dutch republic, Portugal, and others joined together to prevent the union of the French and Spanish thrones

_____ 11. Agreement giving Britain permission to send enslaved Africans to Spain's American colonies

_____ 12. Country considered the military leader of France in the early 1700s

A. Louis XIV

B. skepticism

C. Molière

D. *asiento*

E. Edict of Nantes

F. France

G. Jean Baptiste Colbert

H. Britain

I. Versailles

J. Cardinal Richelieu

K. War of the Spanish Succession

L. intendants

M. Henry of Navarre

CHAPTER 5
Section 3

RETEACHING ACTIVITY *Central European Monarchs Clash*

Determining Main Ideas Complete the chart below by answering the questions about each topic.

Thirty Years' War	1. When did the war start?	2. What two religions were involved?
Hapsburg triumphs	3. Who led the Hapsburg armies in putting down the Czech uprising?	4. How were Hapsburg soldiers paid?
Hapsburg defeats	5. Who drove the Hapsburg armies out of Germany?	6. Why did Cardinal Richelieu send French troops to join the German protestants?
Maria Theresa	7. What was Maria Theresa's affect on the nobility?	8. Which family did she belong to? Which country did she rule?
Frederick the Great	9. Which country did he rule?	10. How did Frederick II feel a ruler should treat his people?
Seven Years' War	11. How did France get involved in this war?	12. Who was the real victor of the war?

CHAPTER 5

Section 4

RETEACHING ACTIVITY *Absolute Rulers of Russia*

Multiple Choice Choose the best answer for each item. Write the letter of your answer in the blank.

_____ 1. Ivan III of Russia accomplished all of the following *except*
   a. establishing a policy of Russian isolationism.
   b. centralizing the Russia government.
   c. liberating Russia from the Mongols.
   d. conquering much of the territory around Moscow.

_____ 2. Ivan IV took the title of
   a. Caesar.
   b. emperor.
   c. king.
   d. czar.

_____ 3. Russia's landowning wealthy were known as
   a. serfs.
   b. nobles.
   c. boyars.
   d. czars.

_____ 4. A grandnephew of Ivan the Terrible's wife, Anastasia, started the
   a. Romanov dynasty.
   b. Hapsburg dynasty.
   c. Russian Revolution.
   d. westernization of Russia.

_____ 5. One of Russia's greatest reformers was
   a. Ivan III.
   b. Peter the Great.
   c. Anastasia.
   d. Ivan the Terrible.

_____ 6. Peter I believed that Russia's prosperity depended on its having
   a. a strong army.
   b. a warm-water port.
   c. a strong czar.
   d. advanced technology.

_____ 7. Peter increased his power as an absolute ruler by all of the following methods *except*
   a. abolishing the office of patriarch.
   b. reducing the power of the landowners.
   c. modernizing the army.
   d. banning people from leaving the country.

_____ 8. Which city gave Russia the "window on the sea" that Peter wanted?
   a. Kiev
   b. Moscow
   c. St. Petersburg
   d. Novgorod

CHAPTER
5
Section 5

RETEACHING ACTIVITY *Parliament Limits the English Monarchy*

Determining Main Ideas Choose the word that most accurately completes each sentence below. Write that word in the blank provided.

habeas corpus	Charles I	cabinet
English Civil War	constitutional monarchy	Tories
prime minister	Parliament	Restoration
James II	Oliver Cromwell	Whigs
James I		

1. He became king of England upon Elizabeth I's death: _____

2. Main cause of conflict with English monarchs in the late 1600s: _____

3. Monarch who dissolved Parliament in 1629: _____

4. Struggle between the Cavaliers and the Roundheads in England: _____

5. General who led the Puritan attack on Charles I: _____

6. Name for the period of Charles II's reign after Cromwell died: _____

7. Law passed by Parliament that gave a prisoner the right to have a judge specify the charges against him or her: _____

8. Ancestors of England's first political parties: _____ and _____

9. English king overthrown in a bloodless revolution called the Glorious Revolution: _____

10. Under William and Mary, England became this kind of government, in which laws limited the ruler's power: _____

11. A group of government ministers who acted in the ruler's name: _____

12. The leader of the majority party in Parliament who heads the cabinet: _____

CHAPTER
6
Section 1

GUIDED READING *The Scientific Revolution*

A. Determining Main Ideas As you read about the revolution in scientific thinking, take notes to answer the questions.

How did the following help pave the way for the Scientific Revolution?
1. The Renaissance
2. Age of European exploration

What did each scientist discover about the universe?
3. Nicolaus Copernicus
4. Johannes Kepler
5. Galileo Galilei
6. Isaac Newton

What important developments took place in the following areas?
7. Scientific instruments
8. Medicine
9. Chemistry

B. Determining Main Ideas On the back of this paper, explain how the **scientific method** is based on the ideas of Francis Bacon and René Descartes.

Name _____ Date _____

GUIDED READING *The Enlightenment in Europe*

A. Summarizing As you read this section, fill in the diagram by describing the beliefs of Enlightenment thinkers and writers.

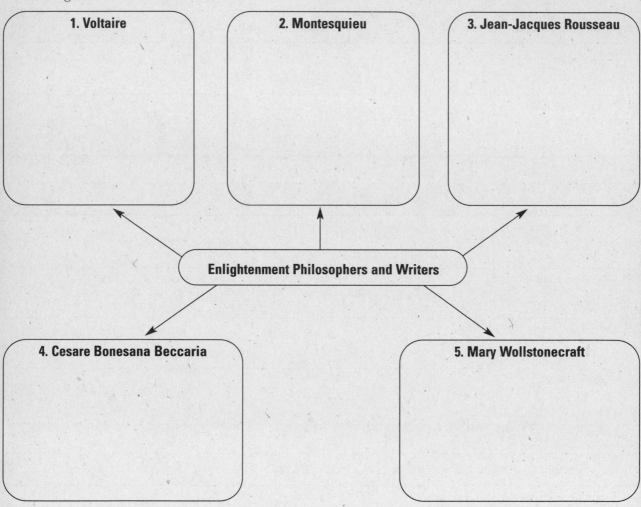

1. Voltaire

2. Montesquieu

3. Jean-Jacques Rousseau

Enlightenment Philosophers and Writers

4. Cesare Bonesana Beccaria

5. Mary Wollstonecraft

B. Drawing Conclusions How did Enlightenment thinkers and writers set the stage for revolutionary movements?

_____

_____

_____

C. Contrasting On the back of this paper, write a paragraph contrasting Thomas Hobbes's **social contract** view of government with the political philosophy of **John Locke.**

Name _____ Date _____

A. Drawing Conclusions As you read about art, literature, and politics in the Age of Reason, explain how each of the following people reflected Enlightenment ideas.

The Arts	
1. Denis Diderot	
2. Franz Joseph Haydn	
3. Wolfgang Amadeus Mozart	
4. Ludwig van Beethoven	
5. Samuel Richardson	

Government	
6. Frederick the Great	
7. Joseph II	
8. Catherine the Great	

B. Summarizing On the back of this paper, define the following terms:

salon   baroque   neoclassical   enlightened despot

CHAPTER
6
Section 4

GUIDED READING *The American Revolution*

A. Analyzing Causes and Recognizing Effects As you read this section, note some causes and effects relating to the American Revolution and the establishment of the United States as a republic.

Causes	Events	Effects
	1. British parliament passes Stamp Act.	
	2. British close Boston harbor and station troops in city.	
	3. Second Continental Congress votes to form an army under command of George Washington.	
	4. France enters the war in 1778.	
	5. By approving the Articles of Confederation, states create a weak national government.	

B. Writing Expository Paragraphs On the back of this paper, write one or two paragraphs explaining how the **Declaration of Independence** and the U.S. Constitution reflect Enlightenment ideas about government. Use the following terms in your writing:

checks and balances   **federal system**   **Bill of Rights**

Name _____ Date _____

BUILDING VOCABULARY *Enlightenment and Revolution*

A. *Matching* Match the description in the second column with the term or name in the first column. Write the appropriate letter next to the word.

_____ 1. Galileo Galilei

_____ 2. Isaac Newton

_____ 3. Enlightenment

_____ 4. Catherine the Great

_____ 5. John Locke

_____ 6. Montesquieu

_____ 7. Voltaire

_____ 8. Mary Wollstonecraft

a. English philosopher who proposed that a government's power comes from the consent of the citizens and that citizens have the right to rebel against unjust rulers

b. Russian empress who was considered an enlightened despot

c. Italian scientist who made astronomical observations that supported the theories of Copernicus

d. early proponent of women's rights

e. English scientist who discovered the law of gravity

f. French philosophe who promoted freedom of speech

g. French writer who proposed the ideas of separation of powers and checks and balances in government

h. intellectual movement that stressed reason and thought and the power of individuals to solve problems

B. *Completion* Select the term or name that best completes the sentence.

| salons | enlightened despot | social contract | Declaration of Independence |
| neoclassical | checks and balances | federal system | Bill of Rights |

1. Under the influence of the Enlightenment, the grand, ornate style in European art known as baroque gave way to a simple, elegant style that was based on classical Greek and Roman ideas and was called _____.

2. A form of government in which power is divided between national and state governments is a _____.

3. The document in which American colonists asserted their independence from Great Britain was the _____.

4. The first ten amendments to the U.S. Constitution are known as the _____.

5. In social gatherings called _____, wealthy hostesses of Paris helped spread the ideas of the Enlightenment to educated Europeans.

6. Thomas Hobbes called the agreement by which people create a government the _____.

C. *Writing* Write a paragraph explaining the following terms and how they are related.

geocentric theory   Scientific Revolution   heliocentric theory   scientific method

Name _____ Date _____

CHAPTER

6

Section 1

SKILLBUILDER PRACTICE *Clarifying*

You can clarify information you read by looking up the meaning of unfamiliar terms and summarizing the main ideas in your own words. As you read the passage below, make notes of the main ideas. Look up any unfamiliar or technical terms you do not understand. Then complete the activities that follow. (See Skillbuilder Handbook)

Galileo Galilei was an Italian mathematician, astronomer, and physicist. As a physicist, he began a whole new field of scientific investigation— the modern science of dynamics.

As a youth of 18, Galileo watched the movements of a cathedral's chandelier as it swung back and forth on its chain. Aristotle had written that a pendulum swings more slowly as it approaches its resting point. Galileo tested this idea and found it incorrect. Feeling his pulse to keep time, he found that each oscillation of the pendulum took exactly the same amount of time.

Galileo's observation led to a new method of measuring time. In the 1200s and 1300s European inventors had built clocks that were driven by weights. In the 1400s, they turned to spring-driven clocks. But none of these timepieces were very accurate. In 1656, a Dutch astronomer built a clock using a pendulum. It proved to be more accurate than earlier ways of measuring time. In fact, pendulum clocks were not surpassed in accuracy until the introduction of electricity.

In addition to discovering the law of the pendulum, Galileo performed other experiments in physics. For days he rolled balls down a slope and measured the speed at which they moved. His data led him to conclude that freely falling bodies, heavy or light, had the same, constant acceleration. He also discovered that an object moving on a perfectly smooth horizontal surface would neither speed up or slow down.

1. Define each of the following terms:

Physicist: _____

Dynamics: _____

Oscillation: _____

2. Identify the main idea of the passage. _____

_____

_____

_____

3. Write a paragraph summarizing the main idea and key details in this passage. Remember to restate information in your own words.

_____

_____

_____

_____

CHAPTER 6

Section 1

GEOGRAPHY APPLICATION: LOCATION
Three Theories of the Solar System

Directions: Read the paragraphs below and study the illustrations carefully. Then answer the questions that follow.

In the second century A.D., Claudius Ptolemy, an astronomer who lived in Egypt, claimed that the sun, stars, and other planets revolved around the earth. These ideas were unchallenged nearly 1,300 years until Nicolaus Copernicus, a Polish astronomer, discovered his revolutionary theory about the sun.

Ptolemy had believed in his geocentric or earth-centered view for several reasons. First, because of gravity all objects were attracted to the earth, which suggested to him that the earth must be the center. Second, he thought that the earth did not move. He showed how an object is thrown in the air and falls in practically the same place. If the earth moved, he theorized, that object should fall in a different place. Even today, these arguments would be difficult to disprove by observation. As a result, Ptolemy's views remained undisputed for centuries.

During the 1500s, Copernicus did not accept the Ptolemaic view. He became convinced that a different explanation of the solar system existed. After 25 years of observation, Copernicus concluded that the sun was the center of the solar system and that the planets, including the earth, revolved around the sun in "perfect divine circles."

Copernicus's conclusion at first went practically unnoticed. However, in the 1600s a German astronomer, Johannes Kepler, supported Copernicus's belief with mathematics. He also proved that the planets travel in ellipses (ovals), not perfect circles, around the sun. Both Copernicus's and Kepler's breakthroughs laid the foundation of modern day knowledge of the solar system.

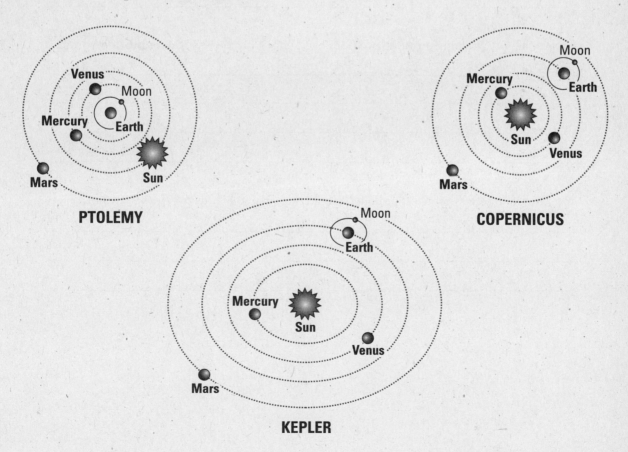

PTOLEMY

COPERNICUS

KEPLER

Interpreting Text and Visuals

1. What object did Ptolemy claim was at the center of the universe? _____

2. What object did Copernicus conclude was actually at the center of the universe? _____

3. What object is farthest from the center in all three systems? _____

4. What object is closest to the earth in all three systems? _____

_____

5. According to Ptolemy, where was the sun in relation to Earth and the other planets? _____

_____

6. According to Copernicus, what planets are located between the sun and the Earth? _____

_____

7. What is the main difference between Kepler's system and the Copernican system? _____

_____

8. Compare the way Ptolemy provided proof for his theory with the way Kepler provided proof

for his theory. _____

_____

_____

_____

Do you think Ptolemy's proof of his beliefs would be acceptable today? Why or why not?

_____

_____

_____

CHAPTER 6

Section 1

PRIMARY SOURCE *from Starry Messenger*
by Galileo Galilei

In 1610, Galileo Galilei, a professor of mathematics at the University of Padua in Italy, published Starry Messenger. *This book, which made Galileo famous in Europe, described startling astronomical observations that he made with the aid of a new invention, the telescope. As you read this excerpt from Galileo's book, think about the discoveries he made.*

Great indeed are the things which in this brief treatise I propose for observation and consideration by all students of nature. I say great, because of the excellence of the subject itself, the entirely unexpected and novel character of these things, and finally because of the instrument by means of which they have been revealed to our senses.

Surely it is a great thing to increase the numerous host of fixed stars previously visible to the unaided vision, adding countless more which have never before been seen, exposing these plainly to the eye in numbers ten times exceeding the old and familiar stars.

It is a very beautiful thing, and most gratifying to the sight, to behold the body of the moon, distant from us almost sixty earthly radii, as if it were no farther away than two such measures—so that its diameter appears almost thirty times larger . . . as when viewed with the naked eye. In this way one may learn with all the certainty of sense evidence that the moon is not robed in a smooth and polished surface but is in fact rough and uneven, covered everywhere, just like the earth's surface, with huge prominences, deep valleys, and chasms.

Again, it seems to me a matter of no small importance to have ended the dispute about the Milky Way by making its nature manifest to the very senses as well as to the intellect. . . . But what surpasses all wonders by far, and what particularly moves us to seek the attention of all astronomers and philosophers, is the discovery of four wandering stars not known or observed by any man before us. Like Venus and Mercury, which have their own periods about the sun, these have theirs about a certain star that is conspicuous among those already known, which they sometimes precede and sometimes follow, without ever departing from it beyond certain limits. All these facts were discovered and observed by me not many days ago with the aid of a spyglass which I devised, after first being illuminated by divine grace. Perhaps other things, still more remarkable, will in time be discovered by me or by other observers with the aid of such an instrument, the form and construction of which I shall first briefly explain, as well as the occasion of its having been devised. Afterwards I shall relate the story of the observations I have made. . . .

We have now briefly recounted the observations made thus far with regard to the moon. . . . There remains the matter which in my opinion deserves to be considered the most important of all—the disclosure of four PLANETS never seen from the creation of the world up to our own time, together with the occasion of my having discovered and studied them, their arrangements, and the observations made of their movements and alterations during the past two months. I invite all astronomers to apply themselves to examine them and determine their periodic times, something which has so far been quite impossible to complete, owing to the shortness of the time. Once more, however, warning is given that it will be necessary to have a very accurate telescope such as we have described at the beginning of this discourse.

from James Brophy and Henry Paolucci, eds., *The Achievement of Galileo* (New York: Twayne Publishers, 1962), 22–26.

Research Option

Using Visual Stimuli for Writing

Find photographs to illustrate the discoveries that Galileo announced in his book *Starry Messenger*. For example, find photographs of Jupiter's four major moons, the Milky Way, and the surface of Earth's moon. Then work with your classmates to write captions for the illustrations and make a bulletin board display.

CHAPTER 6

Section 2

PRIMARY SOURCE *from* The Social Contract
by Jean-Jacques Rousseau

In The Social Contract, *published in 1762, the philosophe—a writer during the 18th century French Enlightenment—Jean-Jacques Rousseau outlined his ideas about individual freedom and obedience to authority. As you read this excerpt, think about Rousseau's argument against the use of force as a means of governing the people.*

Chapter I—Subject of the First Book

Man is born free; and everywhere he is in chains. One thinks himself the master of others, and still remains a greater slave than they. How did this change come about? I do not know. What can make it legitimate? That question I think I can answer.

If I took into account only force, and the effects derived from it, I should say: "As long as a people is compelled to obey, and obeys, it does well; as soon as it can shake off the yoke, and shakes it off, it does still better; for, regaining its liberty by the same right as took it away, either it is justified in resuming it or there was no justification for those who took it away." But the social order is a sacred right which is the basis of all rights. Nevertheless, this right does not come from nature, and must therefore be founded on conventions. Before coming to that, I have to prove what I have just asserted.

Chapter III—The Right of the Strongest

The strongest is never strong enough to be always the master, unless he transforms strength into right, and obedience into duty. Hence the right of the strongest, which, though to all seeming meant ironically, is really laid down as a fundamental principle. But are we never to have an explanation of this phrase? Force is a physical power, and I fail to see what moral effect it can have. To yield to force is an act of necessity, not of will—at the most, an act of prudence. In what sense can it be a duty?

Suppose for a moment that this so-called "right" exists. I maintain that the sole result is a mass of inexplicable nonsense. For, if force creates right, the effect changes with the cause: every force that is greater than the first succeeds to its right. As soon as it is possible to disobey with impunity, dis-

obedience is legitimate; and, the strongest being always in the right, the only thing that matters is to act so as to become the strongest. But what kind of right is that which perishes when force fails? If we must obey perforce, there is no need to obey because we ought; and if we are not forced to obey, we are under no obligation to do so. Clearly, the word "right" adds nothing to force: in this connection, it means absolutely nothing.

Obey the powers that be. If this means yield to force, it is a good precept, but superfluous: I can answer for its never being violated. All power comes from God, I admit; but so does all sickness: does that mean that we are forbidden to call in the doctor? A brigand [bandit] surprises me at the edge of a wood: must I not merely surrender my purse on compulsion, but, even if I could withhold it, am I in conscience bound to give it up? For certainly the pistol he holds is also a power.

Let us then admit that force does not create right, and that we are obliged to obey only legitimate powers. In that case, my original question recurs.

from Jean-Jacques Rousseau, *The Social Contract and Discourses and Other Essays,* trans. by G.D.H. Cole (E.P. Dutton & Company, Inc., 1950). Reprinted in Peter Gay, ed., *The Enlightenment: A Comprehensive Anthology* (New York: Simon and Schuster, 1973), 322–325.

Discussion Questions

Analyzing Issues

1. Which did Rousseau believe was better—a government freely formed by the people or one imposed on a people by force?
2. Did Rousseau believe that it was the right of the strongest to rule?
3. ***Making Inferences*** How would you compare Locke's ideas about government with Rousseau's?

CHAPTER 6

Section 2

PRIMARY SOURCE *from* *Two Treatises on Government*
by John Locke

*English philosopher John Locke (1632–1704) attacked absolute monarchy and
promoted the concept of government by the people in his most famous work,
Two Treatises on Government. Published in 1690, his book influenced the ideas
of the philosophes Baron de Montesquieu and Jean-Jacques Rousseau as well as
the framers of the United States Constitution. At the heart of Locke's argument
was his belief that all people are born free and equal, with three natural rights:
life, liberty, and property. As you read the following excerpt, think about how
Locke defined one of these rights—liberty.*

Of Slavery

22. The *Natural Liberty* of Man is to be free from
any Superior Power on Earth, and not to be
under the Will or Legislative Authority of Man,
but to have only the Law of Nature for his
Rule. The Liberty of Man, in Society, is to be
under no other Legislative Power, but that
established by consent, in the Common-wealth,
nor but what the Dominion of any Will, or
Restraint of any Law, but what the Legislative
shall enact, according to the Trust put in it.
Freedom then is not what Sir R. F. tells us, *O.A.*
55 [224]. *A Liberty for every one to do what he
lists, to live as he pleases, and not to be tyed by
any Laws: But Freedom of Men under
Government,* is, to have a standing Rule to live
by, common to every one of that Society, and
made by the Legislative Power erected in it; A
Liberty to follow my own Will in all things,
where the Rule prescribes not; and not to be
subject to the inconstant, uncertain, unknown,
Arbitrary Will of another Man. As *Freedom of
Nature* is to be under no other restraint but the
Law of Nature.

23. This *Freedom* from Absolute, Arbitrary Power,
is so necessary to, and closely joyned with a
Man's Preservation, that he cannot part with it,
but by what forfeits his Preservation and Life
together. For a Man, not having the Power of
his own Life, *cannot,* by Compact, or his own
Consent, *enslave himself* to any one, nor put
himself under the Absolute, Arbitrary Power of
another, to take away his Life, when he pleases.
No body can give more Power than he has himself; and he that cannot take away his own Life,
cannot give another power over it. Indeed having, by his fault, forfeited his own Life, by some
Act that deserves Death; he, to whom he has
forfeited it, may (when he has him in his
Power) delay to take it, and make use of him to
his own Service, and he does him no injury by
it. For, whenever he finds the hardship of his
Slavery out-weigh the value of his Life, 'tis in
his Power, by resisting the Will of his Master, to
draw on himself the Death he desires.

24. This is the perfect condition of Slavery, which is
nothing else, but *the State of War continued,
between a lawful Conquerour, and a Captive.*
For, if once *Compact* enter between them, and
make an agreement for a limited Power on the
one side, and Obedience on the other, the State
of War and *Slavery* ceases, as long as the
Compact endures. For, as has been said, no
Man can, by agreement, pass over to another
that which he hath not in himself, a Power over
his own Life.

Activity Options

1. *Summarizing* Paraphrase Locke's definition of
liberty in your own words. Then share your definition with classmates.

2. *Recognizing Point of View* In this excerpt,
Locke refers to Sir Robert Filmer, an author who
promoted the royal view of the basis of governmental power. With a partner, role-play a conversation between Locke and Sir Robert Filmer
about freedom and the role of government.

CHAPTER
6
Section 2

PRIMARY SOURCE *from* A Vindication of the Rights of Woman
by Mary Wollstonecraft

A Vindication of the Rights of Woman, *published by the English writer and reformer Mary Wollstonecraft in 1792, is one of the earliest feminist essays. According to this excerpt, how did Wollstonecraft feel about the education of women?*

I have sighed when obliged to confess that either nature has made a great difference between man and man or that the civilization which has hitherto taken place in the world has been very partial. I have turned over various books written on the subject of education, and patiently observed the conduct of parents and the management of schools; but what has been the result?—a profound conviction that the neglected education of my fellow creatures is the grand source of the misery I deplore; and that women, in particular, are rendered weak and wretched by a variety of concurring causes, originating from one hasty conclusion. The conduct and manners of women, in fact, evidently prove that their minds are not in a healthy state; for, like the flowers which are planted in too rich a soil, strength and usefulness are sacrificed to beauty; and the flaunting leaves, after having pleased a fastidious eye, fade, disregarded on the stalk, long before the season when they ought to have arrived at maturity. One cause of this barren blooming I attribute to a false system of education, gathered from the books written on this subject by men who, considering females rather as women than human creatures, have been more anxious to make them alluring mistresses than affectionate wives and rational mothers; . . . the civilized women of the present century, with a few exceptions, are only anxious to inspire love, when they ought to cherish a nobler ambition, and by their abilities and virtues exact respect. . . .

Yet, because I am a woman, I would not lead my readers to suppose that I mean violently to agitate the contested question respecting the equality or inferiority of the sex; but . . . I shall stop a moment to deliver, in a few words, my opinion. In the government of the physical world it is observable that the female in point of strength is, in general, inferior to the male. This is the law of nature; and it does not appear to be suspended or abrogated [abolished] in favor of woman. A degree of physical superiority cannot, therefore, be denied—and it is a noble prerogative [right]! But not content with this natural preeminence, men endeavor to sink us still lower, merely to render us alluring objects for a moment; and women, . . . do not seek to obtain a durable interest in [men's] hearts, or to become the friends of the fellow creatures who find amusement in their society.

I am aware of an obvious inference: from every quarter have I heard exclamations against masculine women; but where are they to be found? If by this appellation [name] men mean to inveigh [protest] against their ardor in hunting, shooting, and gaming, I shall most cordially join in the cry; but if it be against the imitation of manly virtues, or, more properly speaking, the attainment of those talents and virtues, the exercise of which ennobles the human character, and which raise females in the scale of animal being, when they are comprehensively termed mankind; all those who view them with a philosophic eye must, I should think, wish with me that they may every day grow more and more masculine.

from Barbara H. Solomon and Paula S. Berggren, eds., *A Mary Wollstonecraft Reader* (New York: New American Library, 1983), 267–269.

Discussion Questions

1. *Analyzing Causes and Recognizing Effects* According to Wollstonecraft, what happens when women are not properly educated?
2. *Clarifying* What is Wollstonecraft's opinion of the equality of men and women?
3. *Making Inferences* Jean-Jacques Rousseau believed that a woman's education should primarily teach her to become a better wife and mother. How do you think Wollstonecraft would have reacted to his views?

CHAPTER 6

Section 4

PRIMARY SOURCE *from* The Declaration of Independence

In writing The Declaration of Independence, *Thomas Jefferson drew many of his ideas from the works of enlightened thinkers such as John Locke. As you read the following excerpt from that document issued in July 1776, think about the Enlightenment ideas it reflects.*

When in the Course of human events, it becomes necessary for one people to dissolve the political bands which have connected them with another, and to assume among the powers of the earth, the separate and equal station to which the Laws of Nature and of Nature's God entitle them, a decent respect to the opinions of mankind requires that they should declare the causes which impel them to the separation.

We hold these truths to be self-evident, that all men are created equal, that they are endowed by their Creator with certain unalienable Rights, that among these are Life, Liberty and the pursuit of Happiness; that, to secure these rights, Governments are instituted among Men, deriving their just powers from the consent of the governed; that whenever any Form of Government becomes destructive of these ends, it is the Right of the People to alter or to abolish it, and to institute new Government, laying its foundation on such principles and organizing its powers in such form, as to them shall seem most likely to effect their Safety and Happiness. Prudence, indeed, will dictate that Governments long established should not be changed for light and transient causes; and accordingly all experience hath shewn that mankind are more disposed to suffer, while evils are sufferable, than to right themselves by abolishing the forms to which they are accustomed. But when a long train of abuses and usurpations [wrongful exercises of authority], pursuing invariably the same Object, evinces a design to reduce them under absolute Despotism [a government in which the ruler exercises absolute power], it is their right, it is their duty, to throw off such Government, and to provide new Guards for their future security.

Such has been the patient sufferance of these Colonies; and such is now the necessity which constrains them to alter their former Systems of Government. The history of the present King of Great Britain is a history of repeated injuries and usurpations, all having in direct object the establishment of an absolute Tyranny over these States. To prove this, let facts be submitted to a candid world. . . .

We, therefore, the Representatives of the United States of America, in General Congress, Assembled, appealing to the Supreme Judge of the world for the rectitude [righteousness] of our intentions, do, in the name, and by the Authority of the good People of these Colonies solemnly publish and declare, That these United Colonies are, and of Right ought to be, Free and Independent States; that they are Absolved from all Allegiance to the British Crown, and that all political connection between them and the State of Great Britain is, and ought to be, totally dissolved; and that as Free and Independent States, they have full Power to levy War, conclude Peace, contract Alliances, establish Commerce, and do all other Acts and Things which Independent States may of right do.

And for the support of this Declaration, with a firm reliance on the protection of divine Providence, we mutually pledge to each other our Lives, our Fortunes, and our sacred Honor.

Discussion Questions
Determining Main Ideas

1. According to the first paragraph, what is the purpose of this document?
2. According to the second paragraph, what is the purpose of government, and when do people have the right to alter or abolish it?
3. *Making Inferences* Why do you suppose Jefferson felt that it was not only the right, but also the duty, of a people to overthrow a despotic government? How would the history of the world be affected if despotism were allowed to reign unchecked?

CHAPTER
6
Section 1

LITERATURE SELECTION *from* **The Recantation of Galileo Galilei**
by Eric Bentley

In the 1600s, the Roman Catholic Church taught that the earth was the center of the universe. Galileo Galilei, however, observed otherwise. After publicly supporting Copernicus's theory that the earth revolves around the sun, Galileo was declared a heretic. At odds with church teachings, he was asked to recant, or formally deny, this theory. As you read this play excerpt, think about the consequences of Galileo's struggle with the Church.

Palace of the Inquisition. Galileo's quarters. Guards in the entrance hall. Castelli [Galileo's assistant] is eating lunch from a tray.
Guard. *The Commissar General.*
Firenzuola enters.
FIRENZUOLA, TO CASTELLI. I wish to see the professor alone.
Castelli goes out to a back room where, we can assume, Galileo has been resting. Enter Galileo. The two men stand facing each other.
FIRENZUOLA. Please be seated, Professor. *Galileo sits.* A private conference between the two of us has been deemed desirable before the tribunal reconvenes. Is that agreeable to you?
GALILEO. Has nothing been decided yet?
FIRENZUOLA. I represent the Inquisition. May I use our method of procedure?
GALILEO. By all means.
FIRENZUOLA. I shall begin by sounding you out a little. What is your own sense of the situation?
GALILEO. Do I know what the situation now is?
FIRENZUOLA. Of the situation . . . as it has developed during the hearing. How would you say you were doing?
GALILEO. Not too badly. I nailed down the main weaknesses in Scheiner's [the leading Jesuit scientist] position.
FIRENZUOLA. You maintained—correct me if I'm wrong—that he is a liar. Even a forger.
GALILEO. I proved those things.
FIRENZUOLA. And proof lies very near to your heart, isn't that true?
GALILEO. That is very true.
FIRENZUOLA. Would you expect Scheiner to enjoy being exposed?
GALILEO. No.
FIRENZUOLA. Yet you needed him. No one but he had read your book.
GALILEO. The others could read my book.

FIRENZUOLA. And understand it?
GALILEO. I could help them understand it.
FIRENZUOLA. Between now and tomorrow's session?
GALILEO. The world has waited for centuries for these truths. The tribunal could wait another week or two.
FIRENZUOLA. And in that spirit you have appealed from Scheiner to the six cardinals?
GALILEO. Yes.
FIRENZUOLA. Three of whom, like Scheiner himself, are members of the Society of Jesus. *Silence.* Any comment?
GALILEO. Your own irony is a comment. But not mine.
FIRENZUOLA. You wouldn't, of course, have made this appeal if you didn't think it could succeed?
GALILEO. I wouldn't. No.
FIRENZUOLA. What are—or were—its chances of success?
GALILEO. Oh, about fifty-fifty.
FIRENZUOLA. Yes?
GALILEO. Lucignano's friendly, isn't he? Gorazio and Sordi will jog along behind him, I should think. That's half the tribunal.
FIRENZUOLA. You need five votes.
GALILEO. Are you assuming that the individual Jesuits don't think for themselves?
FIRENZUOLA. What would you assume?
GALILEO. That they have to. Because they respect themselves. And their Order knows about science. . . . They are not inquisitors, they are Catholics, Father Commissar!
FIRENZUOLA. Ah, then you have a better than fifty-fifty chance?
GALILEO. Maybe. If this must be regarded as a gamble. I'd have said faith had something to do with it. You know, the faith which can move mountains.

FIRENZUOLA. Very good, very good. I am not employing our inquisitorial method to torment you. Merely to bring the truth home to you. You have certainly brought home to me your illusion. *Quietly.* Galilei, after you left this morning, the tribunal dismissed your appeal. Unanimously.

GALILEO. What? My book is to be banned?

FIRENZUOLA. Which was inevitable, as I told you in advance.

GALILEO. The tribunal will not even entertain the possibility that the earth moves round the sun?

FIRENZUOLA. Will not even entertain the possibility. *Pause.*

GALILEO. It's unbelievable.

FIRENZUOLA. Tell me why it is unbelievable.

GALILEO. Because what my book provides is not opinion but proof.

FIRENZUOLA. Proof of what?

GALILEO. Of the truth. Obviously.

FIRENZUOLA. The truth. Obviously. Is what is "obvious" to Galilei "obvious" to a tribunal of the Holy Office? Could it be?

GALILEO. Be plain with me, Father Commissar. Proving things true has been my life's business, my personal vocation. Proving certain things true to the Holy Office has occupied me continuously for over fifteen years. The results are in that manuscript. Now if truth did not interest the Holy Office, what would that show?

FIRENZUOLA. What would that show?

GALILEO. A career, a whole life based on a total misunderstanding. A life thrown away. Wasted.

FIRENZUOLA. I should not have enjoyed formulating those phrases.

GALILEO. Then it is so? There is no interest in truth here in Rome at all?

FIRENZUOLA. I am not trying to instruct you but to help you to . . . certain conclusions.

GALILEO, *suddenly.* Do you think you're God? But God could never be indifferent to truth. You can? Firenzuola, you're a human being, aren't you, let me address you as such. Are you totally unconcerned with truth? *Silence.* Then what are you concerned with?

FIRENZUOLA, *unruffled.* What is a Commissar concerned with?

GALILEO, *bitterly.* Power. Just naked power. I suppose that's what you are trying to tell me.

FIRENZUOLA. Let's say administration. A Commissar has very little power. He does what he's told.

GALILEO. By the cardinals. Are you saying they're a lot of power-hungry politicians?

FIRENZUOLA. Heaven forbid! I've got you too excited, Galilei. Let me ask you an academic question. What is a church?

GALILEO. What?

FIRENZUOLA. Not what does it stand for. What is it?

GALILEO. An institution, of course—

FIRENZUOLA. An institution. Among other institutions of this world. Matching itself against other institutions of this world. Matching itself as to what? As to power. Its power against theirs. Or it will no longer exist in this world. What way out is there, except to exist only in other worlds? But the Catholic Church was placed here by Christ Himself. Upon this rock. Upon this earth.

GALILEO. I'm naive in politics, the point is not new. But how, in God's holy name, is the church threatened by wholly unpolitical activities such as mine? How is it threatened by the motion of the earth around the sun?

FIRENZUOLA. I think [Lord Cardinal] Bellarmine must have explained that years ago.

GALILEO. He said all new views were wrong.

FIRENZUOLA. Would that we still had his simplicity! *Pause.* The church is a fabric of traditions, nothing else. None of these traditions must be broken or the fabric as whole would fray, wear through, disintegrate. Now, if Bellarmine could feel that a generation ago, how much more strongly must any good Catholic feel it today! Protestant power was not stopped, as Bellarmine hoped. Throughout Central and Northern Europe, a so-called war of religion has been raging fifteen years, and no end in sight. Not just that, but—

GALILEO, *stopping him rudely.* Yes, yes! *Silence.* But this preoccupation of yours with power and the struggle for power, this disregard of truth and the struggle for truth, this is just your viewpoint, Firenzuola, an inquisitor's viewpoint. The cardinals of the Catholic Church could not, dare not, permit themselves—

FIRENZUOLA, *cutting in just as abruptly.* You appealed to them from Scheiner. Would you now appeal to them from me?

GALILEO. Yes. I reject this "private conference." *Much louder.* Let me go back before the cardinals. Let me set my proofs before the tribunal.

FIRENZUOLA, *gently.* Very good. I can now

complete my report. This morning, Galilei, five of the six cardinals voted for your execution. *Pause.* By burning. *Pause.* At the stake. If, like Scheiner, I am suspected of lying, you may send Castelli to check.

GALILEO. Burning at the stake!

FIRENZUOLA. The verdict was halted by a single opposing vote, but till tomorrow morning only. Hence the decisive importance of this meeting this afternoon.

GALILEO. Not burning at the stake!

FIRENZUOLA. I see you have believed me. *Silence.*

GALILEO, *suddenly.* I have been living in a fool's paradise.

FIRENZUOLA. Had I said so myself, at the outset, you wouldn't have believed me.

GALILEO. My whole life has been based on a misunderstanding. All these efforts, these years, have been wasted.

FIRENZUOLA. And there is very little time left.

GALILEO. For what?

FIRENZUOLA. Even as the captive Arab king can escape the stake by a last-minute genuflection [to bend the knee or touch one knee to the floor as in worship] before the cross, so you can escape it by one small token gesture of submission.

GALILEO. What?

FIRENZUOLA. Read this. *Hands him a scroll.*

GALILEO, *reading tonelessly.* "I, Galileo Galilei, do hereby confess to the sin of disobedience, which sin, however, was committed unintentionally, in zeal prompted by idle vanity, and not in malice as an enemy of Holy Church."

Silence.

And in this way my lifelong attempt to change the church's mind is abandoned forever.

FIRENZUOLA. As you have just demonstrated, your attempt to change the church's mind has definitively failed.

GALILEO. Definitively? Are you the church?

FIRENZUOLA. The Holy Office speaks for the church; the Holy Inquisition acts for it.

GALILEO. No, no, no! I had heard the Jesuits were slippery; I had heard the Inquisition was arbitrary and had not dared to believe it. It's true. But they are not the church. And a final appeal still remains open, the appeal that all Catholics may make when others have failed.

FIRENZUOLA. The appeal to the pope? You have already appealed to him.

GALILEO. The book was snatched from his grasp by the Inquisition. As a good Catholic, I demand the right to present my case to him in person.

FIRENZUOLA. Today? At a couple of hours' notice?

GALILEO. That is for you to say. I don't mind if the tribunal does not meet tomorrow!

FIRENZUOLA. The pope cannot commute a sentence passed by the Holy Office.

GALILEO. Will the Holy Office pass sentence if the pope agrees to state in public what he has already conceded in private?

FIRENZUOLA. Namely?

GALILEO. That the earth moves round the sun.

FIRENZUOLA. That, my dear Galilei, would be more than his triple crown is worth.

GALILEO, *loudly.* I believe in my Barberini [Pope Urban VIII]! I have the right to see him!

Silence.

FIRENZUOLA. I shall try to get you an audience for this evening.

Activity Options

1. ***Making Judgments*** With a group of your classmates, plan, rehearse, and give a performance of this excerpt for the class.
2. ***Analyzing Issues*** As a class, discuss Galileo's dilemma. What will happen if he confesses disobedience? What will happen if he does not confess?
3. ***Summarizing*** Create a playbill, or a poster that announces a theatrical production, for a performance of *The Recantation of Galileo Galilei.*

CHAPTER

6

Section 1

HISTORYMAKERS Nicolaus Copernicus

Earth-Shaking Scientist

"We revolve about the sun like any other planet." —Copernicus, A Commentary on the Theories of the Motions of Heavenly Objects *(1514)*

Watching the sun travel through the sky each day and seeing the stars and planets glide across the sky each night, Europeans concluded that these heavenly bodies revolved around the earth. As a result, they made the logical conclusion that the earth was the center of the universe and did not move. This view also became part of the teaching of the Catholic Church. Nicolaus Copernicus changed all this.

Born in 1473, Copernicus became a learned man. He was trained in Church law, medicine, and mathematics. His main interest, though, was astronomy. After more than 25 years of observations, he reached a startling conclusion: the earth itself moved and revolved around the sun.

In 1514, Copernicus wrote a pamphlet outlining his ideas and passed it around to friends, but he delayed making it widespread. In the 1530s, his views were presented to Pope Clement VII, who had no objection to this new theory. Finally, a former student of Copernicus's persuaded him to publish his ideas. As a result, *On the Revolutions of Heavenly Bodies* became available in 1543, the year its author died.

Copernicus argued that the earth moved in three ways. It spun on its axis every day, it rotated around the sun over the course of a year, and it moved up and down on its axis to cause the change of seasons. His new system put the planets in their proper order: sun, Mercury, Venus, Earth and moon, Mars, Jupiter, and Saturn.

Copernicus's bold idea solved several problems. The order of Mercury and Venus had always been disputed, and his new system settled that. His idea also gave a simpler explanation of the motion of the planets. Because the planets sometimes seem to stop and move backward, the old theory had required a complex structure of circles within circles. Copernicus reasoned that these movements occurred because the earth also orbits the sun. Furthermore, the earth and the other planets orbit at different speeds. His view was not perfect, though. He believed the planets moved in circles around the sun, but it was later proven that they

move in ellipses, or ovals.

Copernicus's theory raised two questions. If the earth moves, why do the stars not appear in different positions? The stars, he said, were so far away that their changes in position could not be noticed. In other words, he suggested that the universe was vast. Copernicus was right, although his argument could not be proven for three centuries. Only then did scientists have telescopes powerful enough to detect that the stars did indeed move.

The second question asked why objects in the air tend to fall to the ground. When the universe was seen as moving around the earth, it was logical to think that objects would fall to the center of the universe. Now that the earth moved, it was no longer the center. However, Copernicus believed that an object tended to fall to the center of its home. Thus, articles on Earth would be pulled to Earth, and those on the moon would be pulled to the moon. He suggested the basics of gravity about 100 years before Isaac Newton.

Copernicus's views did not cause much of a stir at first. Although his idea challenged Catholic teaching about the universe, the Church did not object to the new theory. However, Martin Luther and John Calvin, leaders of the Reformation, both objected strongly. Calvin asked, "Who will venture to place the authority of Copernicus above that of the Holy Spirit?" Over time, though, Catholics objected as well. By 1616, the Church officially called his idea false. The work of later astronomers, however, showed that Copernicus drew an accurate picture of the solar system.

Questions

1. *Determining Main Ideas* According to Copernicus, what were the ways in which the earth moved?

2. *Making Inferences* Since Copernicus's theory was not perfect and could not explain all observations of the heavens, why did some people accept it?

3. *Clarifying* How did Copernicus use the idea of bodies tending toward different centers to support his theory?

CHAPTER 6

Section 2

HISTORYMAKERS Baron de Montesquieu
Writing the Science of Government

"It is necessary by the arrangement of things, power checks power."—
Montesquieu, On the Spirit of Laws (1748)

Charles-Louis de Secondat, the Baron de Montesquieu, studied politics throughout his life and wrote a huge and exhaustive study of government. One of his key views was that authority should be divided. This idea became popular in England's North American colonies.

In 1689, Montesquieu was born near Bordeaux, France. His family had long served in the military and had good social position. He married a wealthy woman who had a good head for business—so good that he often let her run the family estates. When his uncle died, he became Baron de Montesquieu at age 27 and began serving as a judge.

Montesquieu soon became famous as a writer. The *Persian Letters* appeared in 1721 without identifying him as the author. The book was supposedly written by two Persian travelers who visited France and wrote letters to describe what they saw. In this way, Montesquieu was free to criticize and poke fun at French society. The king, he wrote, was a trickster who "makes people kill one another even when they have no quarrel." The pope he called a "conjuror," or magician. Later, Montesquieu was revealed as the author.

Now well-known, Montesquieu moved to Paris and joined in the luxurious court life there. As a result, his fortune dwindled. The combination of financial need and boredom led him to sell his judgeship. He used the money to take a long tour of Europe. He explored art and science and met leading politicians and writers. He also stayed many months in England studying its government.

Upon returning to France, Montesquieu spent two years writing a book on the English constitution. Then he decided to write a detailed study of government. For years he worked diligently, using as many as six people at a time taking notes. In 1748, after 17 years of reading, writing, and revising, he published *On the Spirit of Laws*. It filled more than 1,000 pages and broke new ground.

Montesquieu attempted to make a science of government. His work reflected Enlightenment ideas that people, using their minds, could under-

stand the world around them. However, he was not a radical who urged rule by the people instead of by kings. He was deeply conservative and hoped to maintain the privileged position of the aristocracy. He believed that the king's power was dangerous but thought that a strong aristocracy could check that authority. He admired England because the strength of its nobles limited the control of the king.

Montesquieu also saw human nature as the same around the world. However, he thought that laws and government depended on many factors, including religion, geography, and climate. Good government requires shaping laws to suit local conditions. He thought it was easier for people to enjoy liberty in a mountainous country like Switzerland or an island like England. Islands protect people from attack by other countries. Harsh conditions in the mountains, he believed, lead people to have a spirit of individualism that promotes liberty.

Montesquieu wanted to make sure that no part of the government grew too strong. The best way to preserve freedom, he said, was to divide authority. The ability to make laws, to carry out laws, and to judge laws should rest in different branches of power.

This idea was adopted in the United States when the Constitution was written. Thus, his ideas took hold in a country with traits similar to those of England and Switzerland. Separated from Europe by a vast ocean, the United States was safe from attack. In their rugged landscape, the American people developed a strong sense of individualism.

Questions

1. *Clarifying* How did Montesquieu's circumstances allow him to spend his life writing?

2. *Drawing Conclusions* Why did Montesquieu think that it was a good idea to have different powers checking each other?

3. *Contrasting* How did Montesquieu differ from other writers of the Enlightenment?

Name _____ Date _____

CONNECTIONS ACROSS TIME AND CULTURES
The Search for Truth and Reason

THEMATIC CONNECTION:
CULTURAL INTERACTION

*As you read in this chapter, Enlightenment intellectuals and artists made use of
ideas and styles from classical Greece and Rome. In what ways are classical ideals
reflected in the philosophy, art, and literature of the Age of Reason? Review
Chapter 5 and then answer the questions that follow.*

1. The classical art of Greece set standards of order, balance, and proportion that
   influenced future generations of artists. How are those standards reflected in the
   art of the Age of Reason? _____

   _____

2. The Greeks wrote tragedies about human themes such as love, hate, war, and betrayal,
   and comedies, many of which were satires. How does classical literature compare with
   Enlightenment literature? _____

   _____

3. Greek thinkers in search of truth and knowledge were called philosophers, meaning
   "lovers of wisdom." How did the views of the French philosophes compare with those
   of the Greek philosophers? _____

   _____

4. The Greek philosopher Aristotle invented a method for arguing using the rules of logic.
   How did Aristotle's work lay the groundwork for the scientific method developed
   during the 1600s? _____

   _____

5. In what other ways does the Age of Reason compare with the "golden age" of classical
   Greece? _____

   _____

6. Classical Greece left a lasting legacy in art, government, literature, and philosophy. What
   do you think is the greatest legacy of the Enlightenment? _____

   _____

CHAPTER
6
Section 1

RETEACHING ACTIVITY *The Scientific Revolution*

Determining Main Ideas The following questions deal with new theories of scientific exploration of the mid-1500s. Answer them in the space provided.

1. Explain the differences between the geocentric theory of the universe and the
   heliocentric theory.

   _____

   _____

2. What are two factors that contributed to the rise of a Scientific Revolution in Europe
   in the mid-1500s?

   _____

   _____

3. How did Galileo's work come into conflict with the Church, and how was that conflict resolved?

   _____

   _____

4. List three new scientific instruments that were invented as a result of the Scientific Revolution.

   _____

   _____

Reading Comprehension Find the name or term in the second column that best
matches the description in the first column. Then write the letter of your answer in
the blank.

_____ 5. Aristotle's earth-centered theory of the universe

_____ 6. A new way of thinking about the natural world based on
          careful observation and a willingness to question accepted
          beliefs

_____ 7. Copernicus's sun-centered theory of the universe

_____ 8. Italian scientist whose findings in the field of astronomy
          supported Copernicus's theory

_____ 9. A logical procedure for gathering and testing scientific
          ideas

_____ 10. English scientist who explained the law of gravity

a. Scientific Revolution

b. Galileo Galilei

c. scientific method

d. geocentric theory

e. Isaac Newton

f. heliocentric theory

Name _____ Date _____

Multiple Choice Choose the best answer for each item. Write the letter of your answer in the blank.

_____ 1. The new intellectual movement that stressed reason and thought and the power of the individual to solve problems was the
  a. Scientific Revolution.
  b. Enlightenment.
  c. Great Awakening.
  d. geocentric theory.

_____ 2. The willingness of people to hand over their rights to a ruler in exchange for law and order in society was called the
  a. scientific method.
  b. Magna Carta.
  c. Enlightenment.
  d. social contract.

_____ 3. The philosopher who believed that all people are born free and equal, with the rights to life, liberty, and property was
  a. John Locke.
  b. Thomas Hobbes.
  c. Galileo Galilei.
  d. Baron de Montesquieu.

_____ 4. The group of social critics in Enlightenment France were called
  a. satirists.
  b. philosophes.
  c. stoics.
  d. revolutionaries.

_____ 5. Brilliant French satirist who frequently targeted the clergy, the aristocracy, and the government was
  a. Thomas Hobbes.
  b. Baron de Montesquieu.
  c. Voltaire.
  d. John Locke.

_____ 6. An influential French writer who wrote that "Power should be a check to power" was
  a. Louis XIV.
  b. Voltaire.
  c. Thomas Hobbes.
  d. Baron de Montesquieu.

_____ 7. French philosophe Jean Jacques Rousseau believed that the best form of government would be a
  a. direct democracy.
  b. constitutional monarchy.
  c. dictatorship.
  d. republic.

_____ 8. Women's contributions to the Enlightenment included all of the following *except*
  a. urging women to enter male-dominated fields.
  b. writing about the inequalities between men and women.
  c. running for office.
  d. holding social gatherings called salons for influential people.

CHAPTER
6
Section 3

RETEACHING ACTIVITY *The Enlightenment Spreads*

Summarizing Complete the chart below by summarizing the significance of each of the people, events, or situations to the spread of Enlightenment ideas.

Person/Event/Situation	Significance
1. Diderot's *Encyclopedia*	
2. Neoclassical style	
3. Changes in music during the Enlightenment	
4. Changes in literature during the Enlightenment	
5. Enlightened despots	
6. Frederick II	
7. Catherine the Great	

Name _____ Date _____

Clarifying Write *T* in the blank if the statement is true. If the statement is false, write *F* in the blank and then write the corrected statement on the line below it.

_____ 1. The 1651 trade law called the Navigation Act prevented American colonists from selling their goods to Britain.

_____

_____ 2. The French and Indian War was fought between France and the native population in North America.

_____

_____ 3. The British eventually were the victors in the French and Indian War.

_____

_____ 4. The Stamp Act was passed by Parliament in 1765 in order to force the American colonists to help pay for the French and Indian War.

_____

_____ 5. The Boston Tea Party was the name given to a convention of colonists who were planning official protests against Britain.

_____

_____ 6. The American Revolution began in a skirmish between British redcoats and American colonists on the green in Lexington, Massachusetts.

_____

_____ 7. Paul Revere was the author of the Declaration of Independence.

_____

_____ 8. The Declaration of Independence was based on the ideas of John Locke and the Enlightenment.

_____

_____ 9. The French entered the war on the side of the British in 1778.

_____

_____10. The first ten amendments to the U.S. Constitution are known as the Bill of Rights.

_____

Name _____ Date _____

GUIDED READING *The French Revolution Begins*

A. *Analyzing Causes and Recognizing Effects* As you read about the dawn of revolution in France, write notes to answer questions about the causes of the French Revolution.

How did each of the following contribute to the revolutionary mood in France?	
1. The three estates	2. Enlightenment ideas
3. Economic crisis	4. Weak leadership

How did each of the following events lead to the French Revolution?	
5. Meeting of the Estates-General	6. Establishment of the National Assembly
7. Tennis Court Oath	8. Storming of the Bastille

B. *Clarifying* On the back of this paper, briefly explain why a **Great Fear** swept through France.

CHAPTER
7
Section 2

GUIDED READING *Revolution Brings Reform and Terror*

A. *Following Chronological Order* As you read about the events of the French
Revolution, answer the questions about the time line.

1789 Aug.	National Assembly adopts Declaration of the Rights of Man. →	1. What are some rights this document guarantees French citizens?
1790	National Assembly reforms status of church. →	2. What caused the peasants to oppose many of these reforms?
1791 Sept.	National Assembly hands power to Legislative Assembly. →	3. What political factions made up the Legislative Assembly?
1792 April	Legislative Assembly declares war on Austria. →	4. What did European monarchs fear from France?
Aug.	Parisians invade Tuileries and imprison royal family.	
Sept.	Parisian mobs massacre more than 1,000 prisoners. →	5. What effects did the September Massacres have on the government?
1793 Jan.	Ex-king Louis XVI is executed.	
July	Robespierre leads Committee of Public Safety; Reign of Terror begins. →	6. What was the stated aim of Robespierre and his supporters?
1794 July	Robespierre is executed; Reign of Terror ends. →	7. What were some consequences of the Reign of Terror?
1795	National Convention adopts new constitution.	

B. *Summarizing* On the back of this paper, identify each group below and its
position during the French Revolution.

émigrés   sans-culottes   Jacobins

Name _____ Date _____

GUIDED READING *Napoleon Forges an Empire*

A. *Evaluating Courses of Action* As you read about Napoleon, note the goals and
results of some of his actions.

Actions	Goal(s)	Result(s)
1. Establishment of national bank and efficient tax-collection system		
2. Enacting Napoleonic Code of law		
3. Sending troops to Saint Domingue		
4. Selling Louisiana Territory to the United States		
5. Waging Battle of Trafalgar		

B. *Summarizing* On the back of this paper, write a brief explanation of how
Napoleon gained power in France. Use the terms **coup d' état** and **plebiscite**.

CHAPTER 7
Section 4

GUIDED READING *Napoleon's Empire Collapses*

A. *Evaluating Courses of Action* As you read about Napoleon's downfall, write notes in the chart to explain how each action contributed to his final defeat.

1. Ordered a blockade to prevent trade and communication between Great Britain and other European nations →	
2. Sent an army to invade Portugal and began the Peninsular War →	
3. In June 1812, invaded Russia with his Grand Army →	
4. Entered Moscow on September 14, 1812, and stayed in the ruined city for five weeks →	
5. Raised another army and fought the Battle of Leipzig →	
6. Escaped Elba, reclaimed title of emperor, and fought Battle of Waterloo →	

B. *Clarifying* On the back of this paper, briefly describe the final defeat of Napoleon using the terms **Hundred Days** and **Waterloo.**

Name _____ Date _____

A. *Determining Main Ideas* As you read about the meeting of the Congress of Vienna, fill in the diagram below.

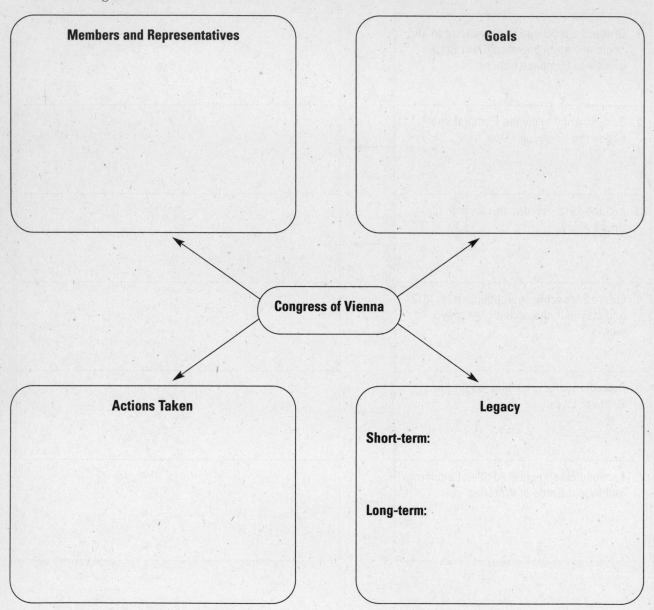

Members and Representatives

Goals

Congress of Vienna

Actions Taken

Legacy

Short-term:

Long-term:

B. *Summarizing* On the back of this paper, briefly explain Klemens von Metternich's efforts to create peace and stability in Europe. Use the terms **balance of power** and **Concert of Europe** in your explanation.

Name _____ Date _____

BUILDING VOCABULARY *The French Revolution and Napoleon*

A. *Matching* Match the description in the second column with the term or name in the first column. Write the appropriate letter next to the word.

_____ 1. Congress of Vienna

_____ 2. Hundred Days

_____ 3. Concert of Europe

_____ 4. plebiscite

_____ 5. Estates-General

_____ 6. Old Regime

_____ 7. Louis XVI

_____ 8. estate

a. one of three social classes in France in the late 1700s

b. the social and political system of France in the 1770s

c. an assembly of representatives from all three social classes in France

d. king of France in the 1770s and 1780s, known for his extravagant spending

e. Napoleon's last bid for power

f. alliance devised by Metternich to ensure that nations would help one another if revolution broke out

g. series of meetings of European powers to ensure the security and stability of a new European order after Napoleon's defeat

h. vote of the people

B. *Completion* Select the term or name that best completes the sentence.

Continental System	Great Fear	Tennis Court Oath	Maximilien Robespierre
Legislative Assembly	Marie Antoinette	National Assembly	Klemens von Metternich

1. The queen of France who spent so much money that she was called "Madame Deficit" was _____.

2. The pledge by Third Estate delegates to meet until they created a new constitution became known as the _____.

3. The first deliberate act of revolution by France's Third Estate was to vote to establish a law-making body called the _____.

4. The Jacobin leader who ruled over the Reign of Terror, in which thousands of French citizens were executed, was _____.

5. The foreign minister of Austria who wanted to restore a balance of power in Europe was _____.

6. Napoleon's blockade of Europe's ports, which was intended to make continental Europe more self-sufficient, was called the _____.

C. *Writing* Use the following terms to write a summary of some of the major events in Napoleon's career.

Napoleon Bonaparte   Napoleonic Code   coup d'etat   Battle of Trafalgar   Waterloo

SKILLBUILDER PRACTICE *Interpreting Maps*

By 1812, Napoleon controlled a vast empire. The map on page 666 of your textbook shows the extent of the French Empire and the lands controlled by Napoleon. To learn as much as you can from this map, study the legend, the compass rose, and the scale. Then answer the questions below. (See Skillbuilder Handbook)

1. Name at least three countries Napoleon controlled. _____

_____

2. What was the extent from east to west, in miles or kilometers, of the lands that

   Napoleon governed or controlled? _____

_____

3. What direction would you travel to go from Paris to London? _____

4. What part of the lands controlled by Napoleon was the farthest south? _____

_____

5. In 1810, Napoleon had signed alliances with Prussia, the Austrian Empire, and

   the Russian Empire. What countries shown on the map were NOT allied with

   Napoleon or controlled by him? _____

_____

6. How does the area of the lands controlled by Napoleon compare to the combined

   area of European countries that were not allied with Napoleon or controlled

   by him? _____

_____

7. What is the approximate distance between Paris and Moscow?_____

_____

8. What were the sites of three major battles the French Army fought between 1805

   and 1809? _____

_____

Name _____ Date _____

GEOGRAPHY APPLICATION: HUMAN-ENVIRONMENT INTERACTION
The French Revolution Under Siege

Directions: Read the paragraphs below and study the map carefully. Then answer the questions that follow.

During the French Revolution, in early 1792, the new constitutional government was under attack by neighboring countries and by opponents within France itself.

Émigrés—former noblemen who had fled France—were plotting on foreign soil to destroy the revolution. They had warned monarchs of neighboring countries that the revolutionary ideas of France were a danger to their own reigns. As a result, Austria and Prussia wanted Louis XVI, the French king, restored. France reacted by declaring war on Austria, which quickly gained the support of Spain, Prussia, and Great Britain. At first, an invading army of Austrians and Prussians moved successfully toward Paris. However, at Valmy the French

government's troops defeated the outsiders, and the tide turned. After that, France invaded the Austrian Netherlands, where fighting was fierce through 1794.

Internally, royalists—local supporters of the king—and conservative French peasants worked against the Revolution in several regions. In August of 1792, the French province of Vendée was the scene of violent uprisings, which spread to other regions. Great Britain even shipped émigré troops to the region to support the royalists and the peasants.

Nevertheless, the government succeeded in crushing most revolts by 1793. The French revolutionary leaders were then able to raise the larger army needed for the external battles ahead.

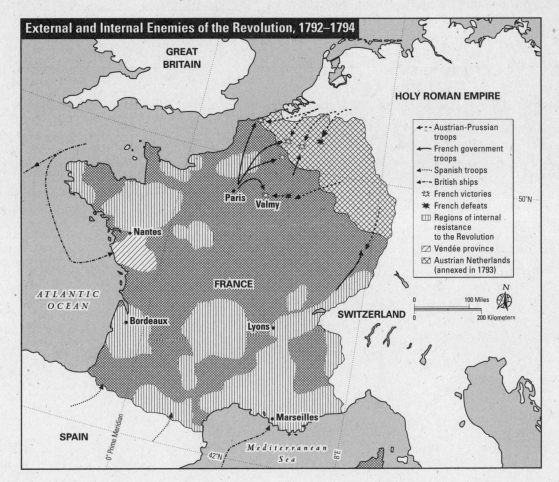

External and Internal Enemies of the Revolution, 1792–1794

Interpreting Text and Visuals

1. What country or countries attacked revolutionary France on land from the south? _____ from the northeast? _____

2. In what part of France were most battles with foreign troops fought? _____

3. How many French defeats does the map show? _____

   Describe the location of each. _____

   _____

   _____

4. Based on the map, what do the French cities of Nantes, Bordeaux, Lyons, and Marseilles have in common? _____

   _____

5. What was Britain's role in the French Revolution? _____

   _____

   _____

6. Describe the events leading up to the battle at Valmy, the outcome of the battle, and the battle's importance. _____

   _____

   _____

   _____

   _____

CHAPTER 7

Section 2

PRIMARY SOURCE *from* A Declaration of the Rights of Man and of the Citizen

On August 27, 1789, the National Assembly of France adopted a revolutionary document, A Declaration of the Rights of Man and of the Citizen. *As you read this portion of the document, consider the rights it guaranteed to French citizens.*

The representatives of the French people, organized as a National Assembly, believing that the ignorance, neglect, or contempt of the rights of man are the sole cause of public calamities and of the corruption of governments, have determined to set forth in a solemn declaration the natural, unalienable, and sacred rights of man, in order that this declaration, being constantly before all the members of the Social body, shall remind them continually of their rights and duties. . . . Therefore the National Assembly recognizes and proclaims, in the presence and under the auspices of the Supreme Being, the following rights of man and of the citizen:

Article 1. Men are born and remain free and equal in rights. Social distinctions may be founded only upon the general good.

2. The aim of all political association is the preservation of the natural and imprescriptible rights of man. These rights are liberty, property, security, and resistance to oppression. . . .

4. Liberty consists in the freedom to do everything which injures no one else; hence the exercise of the natural rights of each man has no limits except those which assure to the other members of the society the enjoyment of the same rights. These limits can only be determined by law.

5. Law can only prohibit such actions as are hurtful to society. . . .

6. Law is the expression of the general will. Every citizen has a right to participate personally, or through his representative, in its foundation. It must be the same for all, whether it protects or punishes. . . .

7. No person shall be accused, arrested, or imprisoned except in the cases and according to the forms prescribed by law. . . . But any citizen summoned or arrested in virtue of the law shall submit without delay, as resistance constitutes an offense.

8. The law shall provide for such punishments only as are strictly and obviously necessary, and no one shall suffer punishment except it be legally inflicted in virtue of a law passed and promulgated before the commission of the offense.

9. As all persons are held innocent until they shall have been declared guilty, if arrest shall be deemed indispensable, all harshness not essential to the securing of the prisoner's person shall be severely repressed by law.

10. No one shall be disquieted on account of his opinions, including his religious views, provided their manifestation does not disturb the public order established by law.

11. The free communication of ideas and opinions is one of the most precious of the rights of man. Every citizen may, accordingly, speak, write, and print with freedom, but shall be responsible for such abuses of this freedom as shall be defined by law. . . .

13. A common contribution is essential for the maintenance of the public forces and for the cost of administration. This should be equitably distributed among all citizens in proportion to their means. . . .

17. Since property is an inviolable and sacred right no one shall be deprived thereof except where public necessity, legally determined, shall clearly demand it and then only on condition that the owner shall have been previously and equitably indemnified.

from Milton Viorst, *The Great Documents of Western Civilization* (New York: Bantam, 1965), 185–188.

Research Options

1. *Clarifying* Use the Internet or another source to find out more about the declaration. Who wrote it? What American document was a model for the French declaration?
2. *Comparing* Read the English Bill of Rights and the American Declaration of Independence. Then make a chart listing similarities to the French declaration. Share your chart with the class.
3. *Drawing Conclusions* What provisions of the declaration forbid conditions that existed under the Old Regime? Consider especially the tax system and the division of society.

CHAPTER 7

Section 2

PRIMARY SOURCE La Marseillaise

Claude-Joseph Rouget de Lisle, a French captain of the engineers, composed this rousing patriotic song during the French Revolution. Because of its revolutionary associations, "La Marseillaise" was banned by Napoleon Bonaparte and by Louis XVIII. Why do you think this song was later adopted as the national anthem of France?

Allons, enfants de la Patrie,
Le jour de gloire est arrivé!
Contre nous de la tyrannie
L'étendard sanglant est levé!
L'étendard sanglant est levé.
Entendez-vous dans les campagnes
Mugir ces féroces soldats?
Ils viennent jusque dans nos bras
Egorger nos fils et nos compagnes:
Aux armes, citoyens!
Formez vos bataillons!
Marchons! Marchons!
Qu'un sang impur abreuve nos sillons!

Come, children of the Fatherland
Our day of glory has come!
Against us the bloody flag of tyranny is raised!
The bloody flag is raised.
Can you hear in the country
The shrieks of those ferocious soldiers?
They come to our very arms
To slaughter our sons and our wives:
To arms, citizens!
Form your battalions!
March forth! March forth!
Let their impure blood water our fields!

from Olivier Bernier, *Words of Fire, Deeds of Blood: The Mob, the Monarchy, and the French Revolution* (Boston: Little, Brown and Company, 1989), 351.

Activity Options

1. ***Making Inferences*** Listen to a recording of "La Marseillaise" or recite the English version of the lyrics aloud. Then share your impressions with your classmates. What mood does the song reflect? How do the lyrics and music capture the spirit of the French Revolution?

2. ***Analyzing Issues*** With several classmates, role-play a conversation among Napoleon, Louis XVIII, and ordinary French citizens.

Discuss why you think "La Marseillaise" should or should not be banned.

3. ***Comparing and Contrasting*** "The Star-Spangled Banner," the national anthem of the United States, was written by Francis Scott Key during the War of 1812. Listen to a recording of "The Star-Spangled Banner." Then discuss with classmates the similarities and differences between the French and American national anthems.

CHAPTER 7

Section 2

PRIMARY SOURCE *from* The Execution of Louis XVI
by Henry Essex Edgeworth de Firmont

Sentenced to death by the National Convention, Louis XVI was executed on January 21, 1793. As you read this eyewitness account of the king's final hours, note the different reactions of Louis XVI, the guards, and the French citizens.

The King finding himself seated in the carriage, where he could neither speak to me nor be spoken to without witness, kept a profound silence. . . .

The procession lasted almost two hours; the streets were lined with citizens, all armed, some with pikes and some with guns, and the carriage was surrounded by a body of troops, formed of the most desperate people of Paris. As another precaution, they had placed before the horses a number of drums, intended to drown any noise or murmur in favour of the King; but how could they be heard? Nobody appeared either at the doors or windows, and in the street nothing was to be seen, but armed citizens—citizens, all rushing toward the commission of a crime, which perhaps they detested in their hearts.

The carriage proceeded thus in silence to the Place de Louis XV and stopped in the middle of a large space that had been left round the scaffold: this space was surrounded with cannon, and beyond, an armed multitude extended as far as the eye could reach. As soon as the King perceived that the carriage stopped, he turned and whispered to me, 'We are arrived, if I mistake not.' My silence answered that we were. . . . As soon as the King had left the carriage, three guards surrounded him and would have taken off his clothes, but he repulsed them with haughtiness: he undressed himself, untied his neckcloth, opened his shirt, and arranged it himself. The guards, whom the determined countenance of the King had for a moment disconcerted, seemed to recover their audacity. They surrounded him again and would have seized his hands. 'What are you attempting?' said the King, drawing back his hands. 'To bind you,' answered the wretches. 'To bind me,' said the King, with an indignant air. 'No! I shall never consent to that: do what you have been ordered, but you shall never bind me. . . .'

The path leading to the scaffold was extremely rough and difficult to pass; the King was obliged to lean on my arm, and from the slowness with which he proceeded, I feared for a moment that his courage might fail; but what was my astonishment, when arrived at the last step, I felt that he suddenly let go my arm, and I saw him cross with a firm foot the breadth of the whole scaffold; silence, by his look alone, fifteen or twenty drums that were placed opposite to me; and in a voice so loud, that it must have been heard at the Pont Tournant, I heard him pronounce distinctly these memorable words: 'I die innocent of all the crimes laid to my charge; I pardon those who have occasioned my death; and I pray to God that the blood you are going to shed may never be visited on France.'

He was proceeding, when a man on horseback, in the national uniform, and with a ferocious cry, ordered the drums to beat. Many voices were at the same time heard encouraging the executioners. They seemed reanimated themselves, in seizing with violence the most virtuous of Kings, they dragged him under the axe of the guillotine, which with one stroke severed his head from his body. All this passed in a moment. The youngest of the guards, who seemed about eighteen, immediately seized the head, and showed it to the people as he walked round the scaffold; he accompanied this monstrous ceremony with the most atrocious and indecent gestures. At first an awful silence prevailed; at length some cries of 'Vive la République!' were heard. By degrees the voices multiplied, and in less than ten minutes this cry, a thousand times repeated, became the universal shout of the multitude, and every hat was in the air.

from J.M. Thompson, *English Witnesses of the French Revolution,* Blackwell, 1938. Reprinted in John Carey, ed., *Eyewitness to History* (New York: Avon, 1987), 250–252.

Discussion Questions

Clarifying
1. How did Louis XVI respond as he faced execution?
2. How did the French citizens who witnessed the king's execution react?
3. *Making Inferences* Why do you think the soldier ordered the drums to beat as Louis XVI spoke from the scaffold?

CHAPTER

7

Section 3

PRIMARY SOURCE Napoleon's Proclamation
at Austerlitz

*Napoleon Bonaparte, emperor of France, conducted a brilliant military campaign
to expand the French empire. After French troops crushed a Third Coalition army
of Austrians and Russians in the Battle of Austerlitz, Napoleon issued this victory
proclamation on December 3, 1805. How do you think a French soldier might
have responded to this proclamation?*

Soldiers, I am satisfied with you. In the battle of Austerlitz you have justified what I expected from your intrepidity [unflinching courage]. You have covered yourselves with eternal glory. An army of one hundred thousand men which was commanded by the emperors of Russia and Austria has been in less than four hours either cut off or dispersed. Those that escaped your swords have thrown themselves into the lakes. Forty stands of colors, the stands of the Russian imperial guard, one hundred and twenty pieces of cannon, twenty generals, and above thirty thousand prisoners are the fruits of this ever-memorable battle. Their infantry, so celebrated and so superior to you in numbers, has proved unable to resist your charge, and henceforth you have no rivals to fear.

Thus in less than two months the third coalition is conquered and dissolved. Peace cannot be far off; but, as I promised my people before crossing the Rhine, I will conclude it only upon terms consistent with my pledge, which shall secure not only the indemnification [compensation for loss], but the reward, of my allies.

Soldiers, when the French people placed the imperial crown upon my head I trusted to you to enable me to maintain it in that splendor of glory which could alone give it value in my estimation. But at that moment our enemies entertained the design of tarnishing and degrading it; and the iron crown, which was gained by the blood of so many Frenchmen, they would have compelled me to place on the head of my bitterest foe—an extravagant and foolish proposal, which you have brought to naught on the anniversary of your emperor's coronation. You have taught them that it is easier for them to defy and to threaten than to subdue us.

Soldiers, when everything necessary to the security, the happiness, and the prosperity of our country has been achieved, I will return you my thanks in France. Then will you be the objects of my tenderest care. My people will receive you with rapture and joy. To say to me, "I was in the battle of Austerlitz," will be enough to authorize the reply, "That is a brave man."

from Milton Viorst, *The Great Documents of Western Civilization* (New York: Bantam, 1965), 201–202.

Discussion Questions

1. *Clarifying* According to this proclamation, what happened to the Third Coalition army in the Battle of Austerlitz?
2. *Summarizing* What did French troops achieve as a result of this battle?
3. *Making Inferences* How would you characterize Napoleon's attitude toward the French soldiers?

CHAPTER 7

Section 1

LITERATURE SELECTION *from* A Tale of Two Cities
by Charles Dickens

A Tale of Two Cities, *written in 1859, is set during the French Revolution. This excerpt from the novel first describes an elaborate reception in 1780 at the home of a powerful noble. Then it narrates what happens when a haughty French aristocrat—the Marquis—leaves the reception in his carriage. As you read, think about how Dickens captures the bitter divisions between the French aristocracy and peasantry and the hatred and inequality between classes that helped fuel the revolutionary violence to come.*

Monseigneur, one of the great lords in power at the Court, held his fortnightly reception in his grand hotel in Paris. Monseigneur was in his inner room, his sanctuary of sanctuaries, the Holiest of Holiests to the crowd of worshippers in the suite of rooms without. . . .

Monseigneur had one truly noble idea of general public business, which was, to let everything go on in its own way; of particular public business, Monseigneur had the other truly noble idea that it must all go his way—tend to his own power and pocket. Of his pleasures, general and particular, Monseigneur had the other truly noble idea, that the world was made for them. The text of his order (altered from the original by only a pronoun, which is not much) ran: "The earth and the fulness thereof are mine, saith Monseigneur." . . .

. . . The rooms, though a beautiful scene to look at, and adorned with every device of decoration that the taste and skill of the time could achieve, were, in truth, not a sound business. . . . Military officers destitute of military knowledge; naval officers with no idea of a ship; civil officers without a notion of affairs; brazen ecclesiastics, of the worst world worldly, with sensual eyes, loose tongues, and looser lives; all totally unfit for their several callings, all lying horribly in pretending to belong to them, but all nearly or remotely of the order of Monseigneur, and therefore foisted on all public employments from which anything was to be got; these were to be told off by the score and the score. . . .

The leprosy of unreality disfigured every human creature in attendance upon Monseigneur. . . .

But, the comfort was, that all the company at the grand hotel of Monseigneur were perfectly dressed. If the Day of Judgment had only been ascertained to be a dress day, everybody there would have been eternally correct. Such frizzling and powdering and sticking up of hair, such delicate complexions artificially preserved and mended, such gallant swords to look at, and such delicate honour to the sense of smell, would surely keep anything going, for ever and ever. . . .

Dress was the one unfailing talisman and charm used for keeping all things in their places. Everybody was dressed for a Fancy Ball that was never to leave off. From the Palace of the Tuileries, through Monseigneur and the whole Court, through the Chambers, the Tribunals of Justice, and all society (except the scarecrows), the Fancy Ball descended to the common Executioner: who, in persuance of the charm, was required to officiate "frizzled, powdered, in a gold-laced coat, pumps, and white silk stockings." . . . And who among the company at Monseigneur's reception in that seventeen hundred and eightieth year of our Lord, could possibly doubt, that a system rooted in a frizzled hangman, powdered, gold-laced, pumped, and white-silk stockinged, would see the very stars out!

Monseigneur . . . caused the doors of the Holiest of Holiests to be thrown open, and issued forth. Then, what submission, what cringing and fawning, what servility, what abject humiliation! As to bowing down in body and spirit, nothing in that way was left for Heaven—which may have been one among other reasons why the worshippers of Monseigneur never troubled it.

Bestowing a word of promise here and a smile there, a whisper on one happy slave and a wave of the hand on another, Monseigneur affably passed through his rooms to the remote region of the Circumference of Truth. There, Monseigneur turned, and came back again, and so in due course of time got himself shut up in his sanctuary . . . and was seen no more.

The show being over . . . there was soon but one person left of all the crowd, and he, with his hat under his arm and his snuff-box in hand, slowly passed among the mirrors on his way out.

"I devote you," said this person, stopping at the last door on his way, and turning in the direction of the sanctuary, "to the Devil!"

With that, he shook the snuff from his fingers as if he had shaken the dust from his feet, and quietly walked down stairs. . . .

He went down stairs into the court-yard, got into his carriage, and drove away. Not many people had talked with him at the reception; he had stood in a little space apart, and Monseigneur might have been warmer in his manner. It appeared, under the circumstances, rather agreeable to him to see the common people dispersed before his horses, and often barely escaping from being run down. His man drove as if he were charging an enemy, and the furious reckless-ness of the man brought no check into the face, or to the lips, of the master. . . .

With a wild rattle and clatter, and an inhuman abandonment of consideration not easy to be understood in these days, the carriage dashed through streets and swept round corners, with women screaming before it, and men clutching each other and clutching children out of its way. At last, swooping at a street corner by a fountain, one of its wheels came to a sickening little jolt, and there was a loud cry from a number of voices, and the horses reared and plunged.

But for the latter inconvenience, the carriage probably would not have stopped; carriages were often known to drive on, and leave their wounded behind, and why not? But the frightened valet had got down in a hurry, and there were twenty hands at the horses' bridles.

"What has gone wrong?" said Monsieur, calmly looking out.

A tall man in a nightcap had caught up a bundle from among the feet of the horses, and had laid it on the basement of the fountain, and was down in the mud and wet, howling over it like a wild animal.

"Pardon, Monsieur the Marquis!" said a ragged and submissive man, "it is a child."

"Why does he make that abominable noise? Is it his child?"

"It is extraordinary to me," said he, "that you people cannot take care of yourselves and your children. One or the other of you is for ever in the way."

"Excuse me, Monsieur the Marquis—it is a pity—yes."

The fountain was a little removed; for the street opened, where it was, into a space some ten or twelve yards square. As the tall man suddenly got up from the ground, and came running at the carriage, Monsieur the Marquis clapped his hand for an instant on his sword-hilt.

"Killed!" shrieked the man, in wild desperation, extending both arms at their length above his head, and staring at him. "Dead!"

The people closed round, and looked at Monsieur the Marquis. There was nothing revealed by the many eyes that looked at him but watchfulness and eagerness; there was no visible menacing or anger. Neither did the people say any-thing; after the first cry, they had been silent, and they remained so. The voice of the submissive man who had spoken, was flat and tame in its extreme submission. Monsieur the Marquis ran his eyes over them all, as if they had been mere rats come out of their holes.

He took out his purse.

"It is extraordinary to me," said he, "that you people cannot take care of yourselves and your chil-dren. One or the other of you is for ever in the way. How do I know what injury you have done my horses? See! Give him that."

He threw out a gold coin for the valet to pick up, and all the heads craned forward that all the eyes might look down at it as it fell. The tall man called out again with a most unearthly cry, "Dead!"

He was arrested by the quick arrival of another man, for whom the rest made way. On seeing him, the miserable creature fell upon his shoulder, sob-bing and crying, and pointing to the fountain, where some women were stooping over the motionless bundle, and moving gently about it. They were as silent, however, as the men.

"I know all, I know all," said the last comer. "Be a brave man, my Gaspard! It is better for the poor little plaything to die so, than to live. It has died in a moment without pain. Could it have lived an hour as happily?"

"You are a philosopher, you there," said the Marquis, smiling. "How do they call you?"

"They call me Defarge."

"Of what trade?"

"Monsieur the Marquis, vendor of wine."

"Pick up that, philosopher and vendor of wine," said the Marquis, throwing him another gold coin, "and spend it as you will. The horses there; are they right?"

Without deigning to look at the assemblage a second time, Monsieur the Marquis leaned back in his seat, and was just being driven away with the air of a gentleman who had accidentally broken some common thing, and had paid for it, and could afford to pay for it; when his ease was suddenly disturbed by a coin flying into his carriage, and ringing on its floor.

"Hold!" said Monsieur the Marquis. "Hold the horses! Who threw that?"

He looked to the spot where Defarge the vendor of wine had stood, a moment before; but the wretched father was grovelling on his face on the pavement in that spot, and the figure that stood beside him was the figure of a dark stout woman, knitting.

"You dogs!" said the Marquis. . . . "I would ride over any of you very willingly, and exterminate you from the earth. If I knew which rascal threw at the carriage, and if that brigand were sufficiently near it, he should be crushed under the wheels."

So cowed was their condition, and so long and hard their experience of what such a man could do to them, within the law and beyond it, that not a voice, or a hand, or even an eye was raised. Among the men, not one. But the woman who stood knitting looked up steadily, and looked the Marquis in the face. It was not for his dignity to notice it; his contemptuous eyes passed over her, and over all the other rats; and he leaned back in his seat again, and gave the word "Go on!"

He was driven on, and other carriages came whirling by in quick succession . . . the whole Fancy Ball in a bright continuous flow, came whirling by.

The rats had crept out of their holes to look on, and they remained looking on for hours; soldiers and police often passing between them and the spectacle, and making a barrier behind which they slunk, and through which they peeped. The father had long ago taken up his bundle and hidden himself away with it, when the women who had tended the bundle while it lay on the base of the fountain, sat there watching the running of the water and the rolling of the Fancy Ball—when the one woman who had stood conspicuous, knitting, still knitted on with the steadfastness of Fate. The water of the fountain ran, the swift river ran, the day ran into evening, so much life in the city ran into death according to rule, time and tide waited for no man, the rats were sleeping close together in their dark holes again, the Fancy Ball was lighted up at supper, all things ran their course.

Activity Options

1. **Contrasting** Use a two-column chart to contrast the nobles at the reception with the common people in the street. Look for clues that show Dickens's attitude toward those two groups.

2. **Writing Narrative Paragraphs** Write a diary entry in which you summarize the events after the reception from the point of view of either the Marquis, Defarge, or one of the "cowed" persons in the crowd.

3. **Writing for a Specific Purpose** Create a sympathy card for the child's family. Include appropriate visual images and a suitable message.

4. **Clarifying** With a group of classmates, perform a dramatic scene based on this excerpt. Then discuss how Dickens shows the attitude of Monseigneur toward his guests or of the Marquis toward the common people of the Third Estate.

CHAPTER
7

Section 1

HISTORYMAKERS Marie Antoinette
Tragic Queen

*"Monsieur, I beg your pardon. I did not do it on purpose."— Marie Antoinette's
last words, apologizing to her executioner for stepping on his foot, 1793*

In 1781, Marie Antoinette, queen of France, gave birth to a son. The king, Louis XVI, now had a male heir. The French people celebrated, as the line of succession to the throne was now secure. A group of poor working women—called market-women—came to the palace to congratulate the queen.

Eight years later, another group of market-women came to the palace. But on this 1789 visit, the crowd was larger and angrier. Instead of celebrating joyful news, it woke the queen with such shouted threats as "We'll wring her neck!" and "We'll tear her heart out!"

Actually, the 1781 visit marked one of the few times that Queen Marie Antoinette enjoyed any popularity in France. Born in 1755, she was the fifteenth child of Francis I and Maria Theresa, rulers of the Holy Roman Empire. The French and the Austrians ended their long hostility by agreeing to a marriage that united the two royal families. Marie married Louis, heir to the French throne, in 1770. She was only 14 years old, and he only 15 years old. Just four years later, the young couple became king and queen of France.

It wasn't long before Marie Antoinette became the focus of nasty gossip and rumors. People saw her as a spendthrift who meddled in politics. Pamphlets portrayed a queen who lived a life of immorality and luxury.

At the same time, the queen was having difficulty adjusting to her new home. Although she and Louis grew to love each other, their early years included many strains. In addition, the queen found French customs confusing. The court had elaborate rules of etiquette for everything from dressing to eating. She had little patience for these formalities, which won her few friends at court.

Marie Antoinette's spending habits didn't earn her much admiration, either. She bought three or four new dresses every week. However, even when she did not spend, she was criticized. In a complicated plot, some members of the court pretended to buy a diamond necklace worth a fortune. When the scandal erupted, the queen—who was entirely innocent—was nevertheless blamed for it.

The people's anger at the queen boiled over during the French Revolution. The crowd often focused its rage on her. In 1789, when the market-women marched on the palace crying for bread, they were calm at first. The next morning, though, they stormed the queen's bedroom, shouting their bloody threats. Later that day Marie Antoinette faced the mob. She stood on a balcony before the crowd, with muskets aimed at her. She bravely remained still until the muskets were lowered. Then she entered the palace.

After the royal family was taken to Paris, the king and queen feared for their safety. Austria and Spain refused to do anything to help. Marie Antoinette urged that the family try to escape. On June 20, 1791, the family attempted to leave but were captured and returned to Paris. An eyewitness wrote that in the city, the queen "was greeted with violent expressions of disapproval."

The next year, the monarchy was formally overthrown and the king and queen were put in prison. A year later, Marie Antoinette's children were taken from her, and she was placed in a separate cell. She was moved again in September 1793 to a small room lit only by a lantern outside.

The queen was taken to trial the following month. She was accused of conspiring to aid her brother—now the Holy Roman Emperor—to defeat France. She was also accused of immorality. She gave a brief, forceful defense that won sympathy. But the officer presiding over the trial warned the crowd to be quiet and then quickly led the panel to declare her guilty. On October 16, 1793, Marie Antoinette was beheaded.

Questions

1. ***Clarifying*** What factors cost the queen support?
2. ***Recognizing Effects*** Do you think the attacks on the queen contributed to the Revolution? Explain.
3. ***Drawing Conclusions*** Would you say that the queen was a strong or a weak person? Explain.

CHAPTER 7

Section 2

HISTORYMAKERS # Maximilien Robespierre
Master and Victim of the Terror

"Liberty cannot be secured unless criminals lose their heads."—Maximilien Robespierre, 1794

For a brief time, Maximilien François Marie Isidore de Robespierre ruled France. A passionate believer in equality, he kept a copy of Rousseau's *The Social Contract* by his bedside. As a religious man, he hoped to create a republic made virtuous through citizens' devotion to God. But despite his belief in equality and morality, Robespierre plunged France into the bloody Reign of Terror.

Robespierre was born in the city of Arras in 1758. He studied the ideas of the Enlightenment and developed strong principles of social justice. He followed the family tradition by practicing law.

Robespierre was elected to the Estates-General in 1789 and thus became involved in the French Revolution. Soft-spoken, he was ignored at first. Eventually, though, his radical opinions won him attention. One leader said, "That man will go far. He believes what he says." The next year, Robespierre was elected president of the Jacobin Club, a radical group that favored the establishment of a republic. Robespierre lived simply and was clearly a man of deep morality. Supporters called him "the Incorruptible."

Robespierre's views on republican government found little support early in the Revolution. However, after 1792, the king was deposed and a National Convention was elected to draft a new constitution and to rule France during the process. Robespierre was elected as a representative of Paris. He became a spokesman for the radical Jacobin group and contributed to the bitter controversies that arose in the National Convention.

As the combination of foreign war and civil lawlessness brought matters to a crisis, the Committee of Public Safety was formed—with Robespierre one of its most dominant members. Under the rule of this powerful group, civil war was avoided and the French army began to win victories.

However, Robespierre and his allies on the committee still faced political opposition at home. In early 1794, he set out to eliminate the Hébertists. This group wanted strict economic policies and an anti-religious campaign that Robespierre could

not support. The leaders were executed. Next Robespierre attacked a moderate group called the Indulgents, who were led by Georges Danton, once a close friend of his. The Indulgents believed that the crisis was past and the Terror could end. They, too, were tried and executed. As Danton was taken to his death, he uttered a warning: "Robespierre is bound to follow me."

After the death of Danton, Robespierre and the Committee of Public Safety—now completely in control of the government—made new rules. They broadened the definition of public enemies and narrowed the penalty to one punishment only: death. The trial process was speeded up. Defense lawyers and witnesses were no longer needed. Because of these changes, 1,500 people were executed in June and July of 1794.

"Fear was on every side, in the creak of a door, an exclamation, a breath," wrote one observer. On July 26, Robespierre spoke before the Convention and said that more people would have to be executed as enemies of the Republic. He only named one man, Pierre Joseph Cambon, the Superintendent of Finance, who bravely took the floor in his own defense. "It is time to tell the whole truth," he declared. "One man alone is paralyzing the will of the National Convention. *And that man is Robespierre*." Others, fearing that they would be accused next, joined to denounce Robespierre.

The next day, in a chaotic scene, the deputies voted to arrest Robespierre and his closest allies. He and more than 20 of his supporters were taken to the Place de la Revolution and executed. A newspaper commented, "We are all throwing ourselves into each other's arms. The tyrant is dead."

Questions

1. *Making Inferences* What about Robespierre might have appealed to others?
2. *Drawing Conclusions* Why did Robespierre eliminate the Hébertists and the Indulgents?
3. *Recognizing Effects* How did Robespierre's methods turn against him?

CHAPTER **7** Section 2

CONNECTIONS ACROSS TIME AND CULTURES
Comparing Revolutions in America and France

Because revolutions have occurred so often, historians have tried to identify some common stages that revolutions follow. Study the stages below from Preface to History *by Carl Gustavson. After reading examples from the American Revolution, give similar examples from the French Revolution.*

STAGE	AMERICAN	FRENCH
1. *Writers denounce existing conditions and provide new goals and ideas.*	Colonial lawyers protested the Stamp Act, and leaders encouraged conflict with British authorities.	
2. *Public discontent results in riots and other acts of violence.*	Colonists engaged in protests and boycotts, including the Boston Tea Party.	
3. *The ruling group is frightened into making repeated concessions until power is transferred.*	British Parliament repealed the Stamp Act; Britain fought the colonists and lost.	
4. *The reformers carry out their reforms, but if their measures are drastic, the nation splits into rival groups.*	The weak national government led to Shays's rebellion.	
5. *Radicals seize power from moderates and try to impose their views on the nation.*	Colonial leaders created a new constitution and a new system of government.	
6. *The public tires of the radicals, and moderates regain power.*	Moderates gained the addition of a Bill of Rights to the Constitution.	

From your answers, what similarities and differences do you see in the American and French revolutions?

_____

_____

CHAPTER 7

Section 2

SCIENCE & TECHNOLOGY
Science Helps Create the Metric System

Though one of the French Revolution's most famous inventions, the guillotine, was designed for executions, another technological development from this period made a great contribution to the future of science.

In 1790, the drive to reform French society moved the newly formed National Assembly to change the way measurements were made. The French Academy of Sciences was asked to develop a standard system of measurement. Up to this point, every country possessed its own procedure for measuring, which often grew out of local customs. At one time in England, for example, an inch was defined as the length of "three barleycorns, round and dry." The problem was that the size of an inch was different with every handful of barley.

The mathematicians and astronomers in the Academy of Sciences wanted to devise a measuring system that would be used in all countries. Therefore, the scientists needed to create a uniform unit of length. They decided to use a certain fraction of the distance around the earth. The

meter—its name taken from the Greek word *metron*, meaning "measure"—was established as one 10-millionth of the distance from the North Pole to the equator along the meridian passing through Paris.

Determining the length of this meridian required surveying the distance from Dunkirk, France, to Barcelona, Spain, which is over 600 miles. Measurements needed to be precise, and the best instruments available were used. The measuring rods were 12 feet long, made of platinum, and equipped with devices to record expansion and contraction due to changes in temperature. An instrument with rotating telescopic sights, developed by Étienne Lenoir in 1784, enabled the teams of surveyors to make highly accurate angle measurements.

The National Convention officially adopted the metric system in 1795. On June 22, 1799, a meter-long platinum rod and a platinum cylinder weighing one kilogram were deposited in the French National Archives as official standards. The government then established a period of transition to the new system, which lasted until 1840, when using the new standards became a requirement.

Over the years, the original measurement standards have been updated to be more precise, and other units have been added. Today, the metric system is the basic system of measurement in almost all the countries of the world.

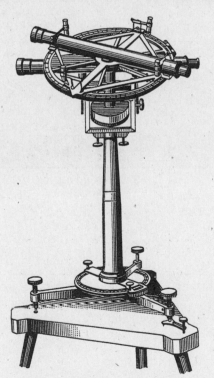

Complex angle measurements were made on Lenoir's instrument, shown above. The rotating telescopic sights are located on top of the device.

Questions
1. *Clarifying* What was the length of the meter as established by the French Academy of Sciences?
2. *Making Inferences* Why do you think the scientists in the Academy of Sciences wanted their new system of measurement to be used in all countries?
3. *Drawing Conclusions* Why was the distance from the North Pole to the equator a good distance on which to base a uniform unit of length?

The French Revolution and Napoleon 67

CHAPTER

7

Section 1

RETEACHING ACTIVITY *The French Revolution Begins*

Clarifying Write *T* in the blank if the statement is true. If the statement is false, write *F* in the blank and then write the corrected statement on the line below it.

____ 1. Under the Old Regime in France in the 1770s, the people of France were divided into three social classes called estates.

_____

____ 2. Most people fell into the Second Estate during the Old Regime.

_____

____ 3. Peasants were the largest group in the First Estate.

_____

____ 4. The Estates-General was an assembly of representatives from all three classes.

_____

____ 5. The Tennis Court Oath was an agreement of Third Estate delegates to the National Assembly to meet until they had drawn up a new constitution.

_____

Determining Main Ideas Complete the graphic by filling in details describing each of the three estates in French society.

Old Regime

First Estate	Second Estate	Third Estate
6. Made up of:	8. Made up of:	10. Made up of:
7. Attitude toward Enlightenment Ideas:	9. Attitude toward Enlightenment Ideas:	11. Attitude toward Enlightenment Ideas:

RETEACHING ACTIVITY *Revolution Brings Reform and Terror*

Reading Comprehension Find the name or term in the second column that best matches the description in the first column. Then write the letter of your answer in the blank.

_____ 1. Statement of revolutionary ideals adopted by National Assembly

_____ 2. Slogan for members of the French Revolution

_____ 3. New law-making body created by the constitution adopted in 1791 by the National Assembly

_____ 4. Members of this law-making body who opposed the idea of monarchy and wanted sweeping governmental change

_____ 5. Term used to describe nobles who had fled France and who hoped to restore the Old Regime

_____ 6. Device used as a means of execution during the French Revolution

_____ 7. Parisian workers who wanted extremely radical change in government

_____ 8. Radical political organization that in September 1792 abolished the monarchy and declared France a republic

_____ 9. Became leader of the Committee of Public Safety and ruled France virtually as a dictator

_____ 10. Period of time during which Maximilien Robespierre governed France

_____ 11. Well-known Jacobin and lawyer eventually executed for being less radical than Robespierre

_____ 12. Executive body created in 1795 as part of a new plan of government

A. Liberty, Equality, Fraternity

B. guillotine

C. radicals

D. Jacobins

E. Directory

F. Reign of Terror

G. Declaration of the Rights of Man and of the Citizen

H. Georges Danton

I. émigrés

K. Legislative Assembly

L. conservatives

M. sans-culottes

CHAPTER
7
Section 3

RETEACHING ACTIVITY *Napoleon Forges an Empire*

Determining Main Ideas The following questions deal with Napoleon's expanding empire. Answer them in the space provided.

1. Under what circumstances did Napoleon become known as a hero of the French republic?

   _____

2. How did conditions in France in 1799 make it possible for Napoleon to seize power?

   _____

3. What is a sudden seizure of power like Napoleon's called?

   _____

4. How did the plebiscite in 1800 affect Napoleon's power?

   _____

   _____

5. How did Napoleon go about establishing order in France?

   _____

   _____

6. What were the terms of the concordat, the agreement between Napoleon and Pope Pius VII?

   _____

   _____

7. What was the Napoleonic Code?

   _____

   _____

8. What incident at Napoleon's crowning as emperor clearly established Napoleon as more powerful than the Church?

   _____

   _____

CHAPTER 7
Section 4

RETEACHING ACTIVITY *Napoleon's Empire Collapses*

Multiple Choice Choose the best answer for each item. Write the letter of your answer in the blank.

_____ 1. The main reason Napoleon divorced Josephine and married Marie Louise of Austria was because
   a. Josephine interfered with his decisions as emperor.
   b. he was seeking a male heir to the throne.
   c. he wanted an alliance with Austria.
   d. Marie Louise was a grandniece of Marie Antoinette.

_____ 2. To prevent trade and communication between Great Britain and other European nations, Napoleon set up
   a. a plebiscite.
   b. a boycott.
   c. an embargo.
   d a blockade.

_____ 3. Napoleon's policy called the Continental System was created to
   a. make continental Europe more self-sufficient.
   b. make trade between Europe and other continents easier.
   c. control smuggling along France's coast.
   d. increase trade with Great Britain.

_____ 4. The war between Spain and France in the early 1800s was known as the
   a. Thirty Years' War.
   b. civil war.
   c. Hundred Days.
   d. Peninsular War.

_____ 5. The Russian practice of burning fields and slaughtering livestock to prevent invading French troops from having access to them was called
   a. guerrilla warfare.
   b. slash-and-burn.
   c. the scorched-earth policy.
   d. the Continental System.

_____ 6. All of the following were factors in Napoleon's downfall *except*
   a. his invasion of Russia in 1812.
   b. his use of the Continental System.
   c. his war with Spain.
   d. the Battle of Waterloo.

_____ 7. The Battle of Waterloo was between the French and
   a. the British.
   b. the British and the Spanish.
   c. the British and the Prussians.
   d. the British and the Austrians.

_____ 8. The Hundred Days refers to
   a. Napoleon's last bid for power.
   b. the length of the Peninsular War.
   c. the length of time Napoleon was exiled.
   d. the length of Napoleon's reign.

CHAPTER
7
Section 5

RETEACHING ACTIVITY *The Congress of Vienna*

Sentence Completion Select the name or term that best completes the sentence.
Write the name or term in the blank.

absolute monarchs	legitimacy	nationalism
balance of power	Holy Alliance	Mexico
Austria	Concert of Europe	Congress of Vienna
Klemens von Metternich	constitutional monarchies	Germany

1. _____ was a series of meetings to set up policies to establish
   security and stability in Europe after Napoleon's defeat.

2. The powerful foreign minister of Austria during the meetings of the five great
   powers of Europe was _____.

3. The idea of keeping the countries of Europe relatively equal in terms of strength
   was called the _____.

4. The country that dominated the German Confederation was _____.

5. The idea that the rulers of Europe whom Napoleon had driven from power
   should be restored to their thrones was based on the principle of

   _____.

6. After the Congress of Vienna, Britain and France had _____ as a
   form of government.

7. The agreement between Czar Alexander, Francis I of Austria, and King
   Frederick William III of Prussia to base their governments on Christian
   principles was called the _____.

8. The _____ was a series of European alliances that assured that
   countries would help each other if any revolutions occurred.

9. One indirect effect of the Congress of Vienna was revolution and eventual
   independence from Spain in _____.

10. Another effect of the Congress of Vienna was to encourage feelings of
    _____ that would ultimately lead to revolution in some countries.

CHAPTER
8
Section 1

GUIDED READING *Latin American Peoples Win Independence*

A. *Recognizing Facts and Details* As you read this section, fill out the chart below to help you better understand why and how Latin Americans fought colonial rule.

Independence for Haiti

Reasons
1. Why did slaves in the French colony of Saint-Domingue revolt?

Strategy
2. What events led up to General Dessalines's declaration of independence for Haiti?

South American Wars of Independence

Reasons
3. How did events in Europe lead to revolution in the Spanish colonies?

Strategy
4. What tactics did José de San Martín and Simón Bolívar use to defeat Spanish forces in South America?

End of Spanish Rule in Mexico

Reasons
5. What is the significance of the *grito de Dolores?*

Strategy
6. What role did Indians, mestizos, and creoles play in Mexico's independence from Spain?

B. *Writing Expository Paragraphs* On the back of this paper, explain the divisions within Latin American colonial society. In your writing, use the following terms:

peninsulares   creoles   **mulattos**

CHAPTER
8

Section 2

GUIDED READING *Europe Faces Revolutions*

A. *Perceiving Cause and Effect* As you read about uprisings in Europe, make notes in the chart to explain the outcomes of each action listed.

1. French citizens' armies win their revolution for liberty and equality.	
2. Greeks revolt against the Ottoman Turks.	
3. Nationalist groups in Budapest, Prague, and Vienna demand independence and self-government.	
4. Charles X tries to set up an absolute monarchy in France.	
5. Paris mobs overthrow monarchy of Louis-Philippe.	
6. Louis-Napoleon Bonaparte is elected president of France and later assumes the title of Emperor Napoleon III.	
7. In the Crimean War, Czar Nicholas I threatens to take over part of the Ottoman Empire.	
8. Alexander II issues the Edict of Emancipation.	

B. *Using Context Clues* On the back of this paper, define the following terms:

conservatives   liberals   radicals   nationalism   nation-state

Name _____ Date _____

CHAPTER

8

Section 3

GUIDED READING *Nationalism*
Case Study: Italy and Germany

A. *Drawing Conclusions* As you read this section, take notes to answer questions
about nationalism as a force for disunity and unity.

How did nationalism lead to the breakup of these empires?		
1. Austro-Hungarian	2. Russian	3. Ottoman

How did each of the following help unify Italy?		
4. Camillo di Cavour	5. Giuseppe Garibaldi	6. King Victor Emmanuel

How did each of the following lead to German unification?		
7. policy of realpolitik	8. Seven Weeks' War	9. Franco-Prussian War

B. *Recognizing Main Ideas* On the back of this paper, explain how **Otto von
Bismarck** brought about the crowning of King William I of Prussia as **kaiser** of
the Second Reich.

CHAPTER 8

Section 4

GUIDED READING *Revolutions in the Arts*

A. *Recognizing Facts and Details* As you read this section, take notes to answer questions about the artistic and intellectual movements of the 1800s.

Nationalism ushers in a romantic movement in arts and ideas.

1. How did the ideas of romanticism contrast with Enlightenment ideas?	2. How were the ideas of romanticism reflected in literature?
3. How was romanticism reflected in art?	4. How did romanticism affect the music of the time?

Realism in art and literature replaces romantic idealism.

5. What trends or events led to a shift from romanticism to realism?	6. How did photography exemplify the art of the new industrial age?
7. What were some themes common to realist novels?	8. What did realist novelists hope to accomplish with their exposés?

B. *Writing Descriptive Paragraphs* On the back of this paper, define **impressionism** and describe the impressionist painting by Claude Monet on page 703 of your textbook.

Name _____ Date _____

BUILDING VOCABULARY *Nationalist Revolutions*
Sweep the West

A. *Multiple Choice* Circle the letter before the term or name that best completes
the sentence.

1. In the late 1700s, people who had been born in Spain formed the top of Spanish-
   American society and were called (a) *peninsulares* (b) conservatives (c) mulattos.

2. The creole general who won independence for Colombia and Venezuela was
   (a) José de San Martin (b) Miguel Hidalgo (c) Simón Bolívar.

3. The creole general who won Chile's independence was (a) José de San Martin
   (b) Miguel Hidalgo (c) Simón Bolívar.

4. The school of political thought that favored giving more power to elected
   parliaments, but with only the educated and the landowners voting, was called
   (a) conservative (b) liberal (c) radical.

5. The belief that people's greatest loyalty should not be to a king or an empire
   but to a nation of people who share a common culture and history is called
   (a) nationalism (b) realpolitik (c) Russification.

6. The German ruler who was a master of realpolitik, meaning "the politics of
   reality," was (a) Louis-Napoleon (b) Alexander II (c) Otto von Bismarck.

B. *Evaluating* Write *T* in the blank if the statement is true. If the statement is false,
write *F* in the blank and then write the corrected statement on the line below.

_____ 1. Two early leaders of the independence movement in Mexico were Padre Miguel Hidalgo
         and Padre José María Morelos.

         _____

_____ 2. The Junkers were radical Prussians who wanted to form an independent, democratic Germany.

         _____

_____ 3. The drive for independence in Latin America was led by creoles, who were at the bottom
         of the social ladder.

         _____

_____ 4. Camilo di Cavour, the prime minister of Piedmont-Sardinia, worked to unify Italy and
         make it a nation.

         _____

C. *Writing* Write a paragraph identifying the following movements and explaining
how they were reflected in painting.

romanticism   realism   impressionism

CHAPTER 8

Section 1

SKILLBUILDER PRACTICE *Hypothesizing*

Historians develop hypotheses to explain why events happened, what the consequences were or might be, and why the events are significant. Like scientists, they test the validity of their hypotheses against historical evidence. In this section, you have read about independence movements in Latin America. In the chart below, write a hypothesis about the role of creoles in the independence movements in Latin America. Then read the passage below and record three facts from the passage in the chart. Tell whether each fact you recorded supports your hypothesis. (See Skillbuilder Handbook)

In Latin America, creoles took the lead in battles for independence. The creoles had a number of long-standing grievances against Spain. *Peninsulares* held almost all of the high government offices in Spain's Latin American lands. Of some 170 viceroys who held office between 1492 and 1810, for example, only 4 were creoles. One creole aristocrat complained to the Spanish king: that the "viceroys here and their retainers. . . mock, humiliate and oppress us" and deprive creoles of "any honorific office of consequence."

Spain also kept tight control over the economy of its colonies. Merchants in Spanish colonies could trade only with Spain. They could transport their goods only on Spanish ships. The valuable mines of Mexico and Peru were under direct Spanish control, which the creoles resented.

The direct cause of the Latin American revolts, however, was Napoleon's conquest of Spain in 1808. Napoleon made his brother Joseph king of Spain. Many creoles might have remained loyal to a Spanish king, but they felt no loyalty at all to a Frenchman placed on the Spanish throne by force.

Fighting broke out in 1810 in several parts of Latin America. These wars for independence were complicated and confusing, since loyalties were divided. The viceroys and their armies remained loyal to Spain, as did some creoles. Native Americans and mestizos fought on both sides, often forced into armies against their will.

Hypothesis:		
Fact 1:	**Fact 2:**	**Fact 3:**
Does it support hypothesis? yes/no	Does it support hypothesis? yes/no	Does it support hypothesis? yes/no

CHAPTER
8
Section 3

GEOGRAPHY APPLICATION: MOVEMENT
Languages Fuel Nationalism

Directions: Read the paragraphs below and study the map carefully. Then answer the questions that follow.

The languages of Europe are divided into four main families—Celtic, Germanic, Romance, and Slavic. Nationalists, people who believed that people of a common ancestry should unite under a single government, often used common language as a tool to achieve their goal.

In central Europe, the idea of a national language sparked ideas of forming one nation. The German people, though divided into many different states and principalities, became obsessed with national unity. Jakob and Wilhelm Grimm, famous for *Grimm's Fairy Tales,* traveled throughout Germany studying dialects and collecting folk tales in the hopes of creating a sense of German identity.

In southeastern Europe, Slavic patriots began a movement to preserve their cultures and foster national identities. These patriots collected folk

tales, studied languages, compiled dictionaries, and wrote books in their native tongues. For example, in a region that was to become Romania, a man named George Lazar began teaching the history of Romania in Romanian—much to the surprise of the upper class, who still spoke Greek. In addition, a Serb patriot, Vuk Karajich, published *Popular Songs and Epics of the Serbs*, formed a Serb alphabet, and translated the New Testament into Serbian.

However, the efforts of these nationalists to help create a sense of national unity sometimes had mixed results. Germany benefited from the unifying elements of language, as the German people formed one country in 1871. On the other hand, the multitude of languages and dialects of the Slavic peoples in southeastern Europe have probably helped keep these peoples divided.

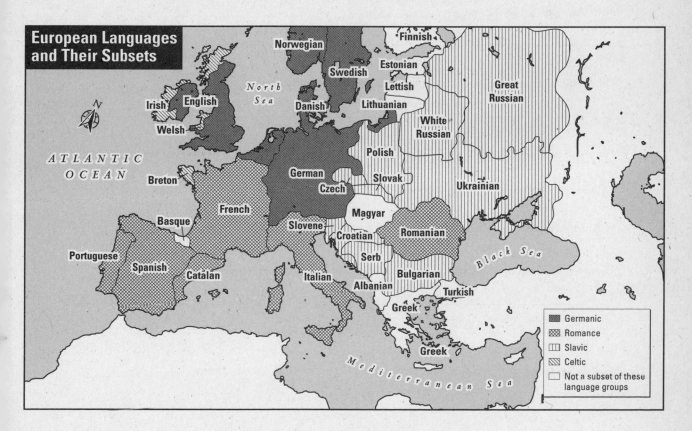

European Languages and Their Subsets

Legend:
- Germanic
- Romance
- Slavic
- Celtic
- Not a subset of these language groups

Interpreting Text and Visuals

1. Name the four major language families in Europe. _____

   _____

   In what part of Europe is each of the language families found? _____

   _____

2. To what major language family does English belong? _____

   _____

3. What part of Europe—eastern or western—has the greater number of languages in one language

   family? _____

   _____

   To what family do most of these languages belong? _____

   _____

   Name five of these languages. _____

   _____

4. What seems unusual about Romania being in the romance language family? _____

   _____

5. How might language help to divide people and prevent them from forming their own country?

   _____

   Examine the map again. In what part of Europe might that have happened? _____

6. How might language unite people and help them to form their own country? _____

   _____

   _____

   Examine the map again. In what part of Europe might that have happened? _____

CHAPTER 8

Section 1

PRIMARY SOURCE *from* Proclamation of 1813
by Simón Bolívar

Venezuela declared its independence from Spain in 1811. However, Spain regained control of the country by July of 1812. Simón Bolívar fled to New Granada—present-day Colombia—to continue the fight against Spain. Chosen to lead an army to drive the Spanish from Venezuela, Bolívar issued this proclamation in June 1813. He appealed to Venezuelans in the city of Trujillo for support in liberating Venezuela from Spanish rule. By August, Bolívar's army captured the capital, and Venezuela gave Bolívar the title of liberator. According to the proclamation, what was Bolívar's mission?

Venezuelans: An army of your brothers, sent by the Sovereign Congress of New Granada has come to liberate you. Having expelled the oppressors from the provinces of Mérida and Trujillo, it is now among you.

We are sent to destroy the Spaniards, to protect the Americans, and to reëstablish the republican governments that once formed the Confederation of Venezuela. The states defended by our arms are again governed by their former constitutions and tribunals, in full enjoyment of their liberty and independence, for our mission is designed only to break the chains of servitude which still shackle some of our towns, and not to impose laws or exercise acts of dominion to which the rules of war might entitle us.

Moved by your misfortunes, we have been unable to observe with indifference the afflictions you were forced to experience by the barbarous Spaniards, who have ravished you, plundered you, and brought you death and destruction. They have violated the sacred rights of nations. They have broken the most solemn agreements and treaties. In fact, they have committed every manner of crime, reducing the Republic of Venezuela to the most frightful desolation. Justice therefore demands vengeance, and necessity compels us to exact it. . . .

Despite our just resentment toward the iniquitous Spaniards, our magnanimous heart still commands us to open to them for the last time a path to reconciliation and friendship; they are invited to live peacefully among us, if they will abjure their crimes, honestly change their ways, and coöperate with us in destroying the intruding Spanish government and in the reëstablishment of the Republic of Venezuela.

Any Spaniard who does not, by every active and effective means, work against tyranny in behalf of this just cause, will be considered an enemy and

punished; as a traitor to the nation, he will inevitably be shot by a firing squad. On the other hand, a general and absolute amnesty is granted to those who come over to our army. . . .

And you Americans who, by error or treachery, have been lured from the paths of justice, are informed that your brothers, deeply regretting the error of your ways, have pardoned you as we are profoundly convinced that you cannot be truly to blame, for only the blindness and ignorance in which you have been kept up to now by those responsible for your crimes could have induced you to commit them. Fear not the sword that comes to avenge you and to sever the ignoble ties with which your executioners have bound you to their own fate. You are hereby assured, with absolute impunity, of your honor, lives, and property. The single title, "Americans," shall be your safeguard and guarantee. Our arms have come to protect you, and they shall never be raised against a single one of you, our brothers. . . .

Spaniards and Canary Islanders, you will die, though you be neutral, unless you actively espouse the cause of America's liberation. Americans, you will live, even if you have trespassed.

from Vincente Lecuna and Harold A. Bierck, eds., *Selected Writings of Bolívar* (New York: Colonial Press, 1951), Vol. I, 31–32. Reprinted in Peter N. Stearns, ed., *Documents in World History* (New York: Harper Collins Publishers, 1988), 89–90.

Discussion Questions
Recognizing Facts and Details
1. What did Bolívar hope to accomplish?
2. According to the proclamation, why were Venezuelans justified in rebelling against Spain?
3. ***Making Judgments*** Do you think Bolívar's policies in dealing with the Spanish and the Americans were fair? Why or why not?

CHAPTER
8
Section 2

PRIMARY SOURCE *Letter to Thomas Moore*
from George Gordon, Lord Byron

*The English romantic poet George Gordon, Lord Byron volunteered as a soldier
for the Greek cause during the war for Greek independence against the Ottoman
Turks. Byron wrote this letter to his friend Thomas Moore, an Anglo-Irish poet,
about six weeks before his death at Missolonghi on April 19, 1824. According to
Byron's letter, what hardships did he face during wartime?*

Missolonghi, Western Greece, March 4, 1824
My dear Moore,

Your reproach is unfounded—I have received
two letters from you, and answered both previous
to leaving Cephalonia. I have not been "quiet" in
an Ionian island, but much occupied with business,
as the Greek deputies (if arrived) can tell you.
Neither have I continued Don Juan, nor any other
poem. You go, as usual, I presume, by some newspaper report or other.

When the proper moment to be of some use
arrived I came here; and am told that my arrival
(with some other circumstances) has been of, at
least, temporary advantage to the cause. I had a
narrow escape from the Turks, and another from
shipwreck, on my passage. On the 15th (or 16th) of
February I had an attack of apoplexy, or epilepsy—
the physicians have not exactly decided which, but
the alternative is agreeable. My constitution, therefore, remains between the two opinions, like
Mahomet's sarcophagus between the magnets. All
that I can say is, that they nearly bled me to death,
by placing the leeches too near the temporal artery,
so that the blood could with difficulty be stopped,
even with caustic. I am supposed to be getting better, slowly, however. But my homilies will, I presume, for the future, be like the Archbishop of
Grenada's—in this case, "I order you a hundred
ducats from my treasurer, and wish you a little
more taste."

For public matters I refer you to Colonel
Stanhope's and Capt. Parry's reports and to all

other reports whatsoever. There is plenty to do—
war without, and tumult within—they "kill a man a
week," like Bob Acres in the country. Parry's artifi-
cers have gone away in alarm, on account of a dispute in which some of the natives and foreigners
were engaged, and a Swede was killed, and a
Suliote wounded. In the middle of their fright
there was a strong shock of an earthquake; so,
between that and the sword, they boomed off in a
hurry, in despite of all dissuasions to the contrary. A
Turkish brig run ashore, etc., etc., etc.

You, I presume, are either publishing or medi-
tating that same. Let me hear from and of you, and
believe me, in all events,

Ever and affectionately yours,
N. B.

from W. H. Auden, ed., *George Gordon, Lord Byron:
Selected Poetry and Prose* (New York: The New American
Library, 1966), 189–190.

Activity Options

1. *Recognizing Point of View* As Thomas Moore,
   write a letter to your friend Byron in which you
   inquire about his health, his poetry, his role in
   the Greek war for independence, and so forth.
   Share your letter with classmates.
2. *Using Sequential Order* Make a time line to
   illustrate what happened to Byron after he left
   Cephalonia. List events that are mentioned in
   this letter in chronological order.

Name _____   Date _____

PRIMARY SOURCE Proclamation of 1860
by Giuseppe Garibaldi

Giuseppe Garibaldi, an Italian nationalist, issued this proclamation before he left on a successful military expedition in May 1860 to liberate Sicily, the first step toward unifying southern Italy. How did Garibaldi try to persuade Italians to fight for Italy's independence?

The Sicilians are fighting against the enemies of Italy, and for Italy. To furnish them with money and with arms, and to bring them the aid of his strong right arm, such is the duty of every Italian. The spirit of discord and the indifference of any one province to the fate of her neighbour are the things that have been at the bottom of the misfortunes of Italy.

The salvation of Italy began on the day on which the sons of the same soil rushed forward to defend their brothers when in danger.

If we abandon these brave children of Sicily and leave them to their fate, they will have to fight against the mercenaries of the Bourbon, plus those of Austria and those of the priest who reigns in Rome.

Let the people of the liberated provinces lift high their voices in championing the cause of their brothers who are fighting! Send your generous youth where the battle is for the Motherland!

Let the Marches, and Umbria, and Sabina, and the Roman Campania, and the land of Naples rise, so as to bring division into the forces of our enemy!

If the towns do not offer sufficient support to the insurrection, let the more determined of you range the country in bands.

A brave man can always find arms! In the name of God, do not listen to the cowards who parade before their richly laden tables!

Let us arm! Let us fight for our brothers! To-morrow, we shall fight for ourselves.

A little band of brave men who follow me on the country's battlefields are marching to the rescue along with me. Italy knows them: they appear whenever the tocsin of danger sounds. Noble and generous comrades! they have consecrated their lives to their country. They will give to her their last drop of blood, seeking no other reward save that of having done their duty, and that a clear conscience may abide with them.

"Italy and Victor Emmanuel!" This, our battle-cry when crossing the Ticino, will echo to the fiery rocks of [AE]tna. To this cry, prophetic of combat, and borne along by Italy's lofty mountains as far as the Tarpeian rock, the tottering throne of tyranny will crash. All, then, will rise as one man!

To arms! At one blow, let us end the sufferings of centuries. Let us prove to the world that it was indeed in this land that the sturdy race of ancient Romans once lived.

from Alexandre Dumas, ed., *The Memoirs of Garibaldi* (New York: D. Appleton and Company, 1931), 359.

Discussion Questions

Recognizing Facts and Details

1. According to Garibaldi, what did the embattled Sicilians need to fight Italy's enemies?
2. Why did Garibaldi think Italians should volunteer to help the Sicilians?
3. ***Recognizing Propaganda*** Propaganda is the use of slanted information to further one's own cause or damage an opponent's cause. What are two examples of propaganda in Garibaldi's proclamation?

PRIMARY SOURCE Nationalist Speech
by Otto von Bismarck

On April 1, 1895, German nationalist Otto von Bismarck delivered a speech to a delegation of students in Friedrichsruh on his 80th birthday. He reviewed key events that led to the unification of Germany and promoted the idea of German unity. As you read part of this speech, consider his hopes and dreams for future generations of Germans.

Gentlemen! I have just heard from the lips of your teachers, the leaders of higher education, an appreciation of my past, which means much to me. From your greeting, I infer a promise for the future, and this means even more for a man of my years than his love of approbation. You will be able, at least many of you, to live according to the sentiments which your presence here today reveals, and to do so to the middle of the next century, while I have long been condemned to inactivity and belong to the days that are past. I find consolation in this observation, for the German is not so constituted that he could entirely dismiss in his old age what in his youth inspired him. Forty and sixty years hence you will not hold exactly the same views as today, but the seed planted in your young hearts by the reign of Emperor William I will bear fruit, and even when you grow old, your attitude will ever be German national because it is so today. . . .

We had to win our national independence in difficult wars. The preparation, the prologue, was the Holstein war. We had to fight with Austria for a settlement; no court of law could have given a decree of separation; we had to fight. That we were facing French war after our victory at Sadowa could not remain in doubt for anyone who knew the conditions of Europe. . . . After the war had been waged everybody here was saying that within five years we should have to wage the next war. This was to be feared it is true, but I have ever since considered it to be my duty to prevent it. We Germans had no longer any reason for war. We had what we needed. To fight for more, from a lust of conquest and for the annexation of countries which were not necessary for us always appeared to me like an atrocity; I am tempted to say like a Bonapartistic and a foreign atrocity, alien to the Germanic sense of justice. . . .

The men who made the biggest sacrifices that the empire might be born were undoubtedly the German princes, not excluding the king of Prussia.

My old master hesitated long before he voluntarily yielded his independence to the empire. Let us then be thankful to the reigning houses who made sacrifices for the empire which after the full thousand years of German history must have been hard for them to make. . . .

I would then—and you will say I am an old, conservative man—compress what I have to say into these words: Let us keep above everything the things we have, before we look for new things, nor be afraid of those people who begrudge them to us. In Germany struggles have existed always. . . . Life is a struggle everywhere in nature, and without inner struggles we end by being like the Chinese, and become petrified. No struggle, no life! Only, in every fight where the national question arises, there must be a rallying point. For us this is the empire, not as it may seem to be desirable, but as it is, the empire and the emperor, who represents it. That is why I ask you to join me in wishing well to the emperor and the empire. I hope that in 1950 all of you who are still living will again respond with contented hearts to the toast.

LONG LIVE THE EMPEROR AND THE EMPIRE!

from Louis L. Snyder, *The Blood and Iron Chancellor: A Documentary–Biography of Otto von Bismarck* (Princeton, N.J.: D. Van Nostrand Company, Inc., 1967), 375–378.

Activity Options

1. ***Recognizing Point of View*** Discuss Bismarck's thoughts about German nationalism with a group of classmates. Then compare Bismarck's ideas with the nationalist sentiments of Bolívar (page 63) and Garibaldi (page 65).
2. ***Using Aural Stimuli*** Deliver this speech excerpt to the class. Try to use a tone of voice and a rate of speaking that will most effectively convey Bismarck's message.

CHAPTER 8

Section 1

LITERATURE SELECTION *from All Souls' Rising*
by Madison Smartt Bell

All Souls' Rising by American author Madison Smartt Bell is a novel about Toussaint L'Ouverture and Haiti's liberation from European rule. This excerpt from the novel's prologue, which is narrated by a French sailor, takes place on board ship after Toussaint has been captured and is being sent to prison in France. Like other Latin American colonies, Haiti was strictly divided into social classes based on birth; the narrator takes great pains to describe the ancestry of Toussaint and his company. What are the narrator's overall impressions of Toussaint?

June 15, 1802   Aboard *Le Héros*

The weighing of our anchor with this morning's tide brought me a lightening of my heart. These last few days we've been in port were most uneasy, owing to rumors of renewed disturbances, perhaps a more serious revolt, to be inspired by the deportation of the brigand chief Toussaint, our passenger and prisoner. All factions in the city of Le Cap or what remains of it are once again aroused against one another. As for the harbor itself, it is alive with sharks, which feed most avidly upon the flesh of those who take the losing part in struggles on the shore.

Thus I was greatly comforted to see us well away, to stand on the stern with the breeze freshening in my face, watching the broken soot-stained ruins sink rapidly enough to the horizon. The town of Le Cap has twice been burned to the ground these last ten years, but even at the height of its ostentation it could not, when seen at such a distance, have seemed any more than a most precarious foothold on this savage shore. Rounding the cape, I see that city give way to rocky escarpments plunging vertically into the waves, and above these the incomprehensible blankness of the forests or, where the trees are cut, the peaks standing out as bare and sharp as needles' points. My sojourn here was brief but more than long enough to satisfy me. Here no enterprise has managed to achieve a good result— the hand of civilized man has done no more than make of a wilderness a desert. Perhaps before Columbus landed, it was some sort of savage Eden here. I believe it would have been better for all if he had never come.

As we set sail, there stood near me, among my fellow officers of the ship, some members of the company of the renegade slave Toussaint, though that gentleman himself remained carefully sequestered, under guard in his cabin below. The others of his party had so far the freedom of the ship, and I observed them closely as I might, with some thought of indicting their descriptions, though for what audience I do not know.

The eldest (and by far the blackest) of the women is Suzanne, the wife of Toussaint. She is said to be older than he and showed her years, appearing confused at moments, appearing not to know just where she found herself or how she came there. But for the richness of her dress (which was, however, modest) she might easily have been taken for any ordinary household servant in the colony. The three young mulattresses in her train (a niece, a daughter-in-law, and a companion as I gathered) struck me as rather more *soignées,* wrapped in that thin layer of hastily acquired sophistication with which one often meets in women of their type.

The lightest of the men is Toussaint's eldest son, Placide, though as our Captain Savary has suggested there are some doubts as to his parentage, suspicion that he may be an illegitimate child of Suzanne's prior to the marriage (yet Toussaint acknowledges and indeed is said to favor him). His light color may have occasioned this speculation, though often the Aradas, from which tribe Toussaint is extracted, are similarly light or of a reddish hue.

As for the two younger sons, Isaac and Jean, it is plain at a glance that they are full-blooded Negroes. The former wears a most extravagant uniform, every inch of it bedizened with gold braid and rosettes, complete with an enormous sword, the tip of it dragging the boards of the deck, whose bearer appears to have no notion of its use. The hilted weapon seems only to encumber the natural movement of his hands along his sides. With all its meaningless pomp this uniform shows marked signs of wear, hard wear at that, and Isaac seems to sulk inside it—a bedraggled peacock, caught in a rainstorm.

I have heard, from Captain Savary and others, that this uniform was the personal gift of Bonaparte to Toussaint's second son. Placide was presented with another like it, on the same occasion, but no longer wears it.

The eighth and last of the party looks a miscellany of ill-assembled and badly chosen parts, being overly tall, gangly, poorly proportioned and clumsy in all respects, all thumbs and elbows. His neck is elongated, with a busy Adam's apple the size of a garden spade, and, above, his head appears ridiculously small. He rolls his eyes and stutters when he speaks, and his outsized, long-fingered hands creep about all over his person like great agitated spiders the while. This singular creature is Toussaint's valet, known by the fanciful appellation of Mars Plaisir. For the moment, he cannot practice his intended vocation, since Toussaint is held strictly apart from all this retinue, not permitted to see any of his retainers or even any member of his family. A pointless severity, I should think, yet I would willingly be deprived of the attentions of a Mars Plaisir. In almost any European village I would expect a creature such as he to be set upon and stoned to death.

Now the very thought of Europe makes me puzzle at my enterprise, for these notes are addressed to no one, nor could I find opportunity to send them anywhere at all these next six weeks at sea. Yet I continue, for there have been other curiosities this day. At even (his family and retainers being at table below), Toussaint was fetched on deck to take the air, under guard of two dragoons detached from Captain-General Leclerc's expedition. Those soldiers seemed to tower over him, for he is only a small Negro man and unremarkable at first glance, more noteworthy for the incongruity of his dress than for any distinguishing feature of his person. He wore a loose white shirt or smock, coarsely woven and open at the neck, over tight trousers from a military uniform, and a pair of high cavalry boots. There was a kerchief bound over his head, and I remembered hearing that Toussaint affected such a covering, not only in his *déshabillé* but often even on occasions of state.

I had the watch, but the sea was calm and the sky clear, with the first stars just beginning to emerge, and I approached a little nearer. He did

not seem at all aware of my proximity, but stood near the stern rail to stare most intently down at the water (there being no longer any land in view). Not knowing what to say to him, or if I ought to speak at all, I was silent for some minutes before inquiring, what it might be that he was so carefully regarding.

And here the sentinel's attention abruptly returned to his charge, and he undertook to prevent our conversation, but I overrode him, repeating my question and adding to it, whether Toussaint was looking back toward the island of which he had lately been master, and whether he regretted it.

At this, Toussaint turned half toward me and looked at me with half a smile, but without immediately speaking. I suppose he must have gone a lengthy while without much benefit of human discourse. Still, there was a sort of slyness in that smile. His lips were full and heavy, his teeth long and yellow; he lacked an eyetooth on the left side. The jaw long and slung far forward, stretching and lowering the deep oval of his face. His nose was long also and typically flat, but his forehead was high and his eyes, with their yellowing whites, were large and expressive—his best feature. All in all, a most arresting ugliness.

He was smaller than I somehow had expected, standing no higher than my breastbone. His disproportionately long trunk was set on little bandy legs—undoubtedly he would appear to best advantage on horseback. Some grizzled hair appeared at his shirt's neck, and the gray pigtail hanging from under the kerchief was fastened with a bit of frayed red ribbon. I would have put him in the middle fifties. He was narrow-hipped and distinctly thin, though not to the point of frailty—his arms were disproportionately thick and muscular.

He returned my looks, taking my measure also it may be, and then resumed his staring at the water.

"*Guinée,*" he said, but so softly I scarce caught the word at all.

"Africa?" I said, with some surprise.

Of course he was not looking in the right direction, but one would hardly expect him to be a master of geography, outside of the colony. He is himself a Creole and I believe this must have been the first time he had ever been to sea. I found that my gaze was drawn after his; he continued to inspect the surfaces of the ocean for some time before he spoke. The water had taken on a red metallic glimmer from the light of the setting sun.

"*Guinée, on dit, se trouve in bas de l'eau.*" Still Toussaint kept his eyes fixed on the water. *They say that Africa is at the bottom of the ocean.*

"But you are a Christian," I said, for I was again surprised, though it was not the first time I had heard of this belief. One often finds the slavers complaining of it—how their new-bought slaves will fling themselves off the ships in droves, believing that they may pass beneath the ocean to regain their original homes in Africa.

Toussaint glanced up at me with the same sly smile. "Of course I am a Christian," he said, "but I should like to see Africa all the same."

Our colloquy could not continue past that point, for the dragoons quite brusquely led him away. Improbable as it is that anyone aboard should enter into conspiracy with such a one as he, his reputation for cunning is sufficient that his guard evidently has been ordered to permit that he converse with no one.

Unfortunate fellow, I should not suppose him likely ever to see Africa—not, at least, in this lifetime.

It was well past dark when I was relieved of my watch, and in groping along through the darkness below toward my own repose I must pass the cabin where Toussaint was held secure. Going along the passage, I heard a voice coming from behind the door, and (the sentinel having absented himself, perhaps to the jakes) I paused to listen. The occupant was reading in a loud sonorous voice, this passage from the end of Deuteronomy:

> And Moses went up from the plains of Moab under the mountains of Nebo, to the top of Pisgah, that is over against Jericho. And the Lord showed him all the land of Gilead, unto Dan.
>
> And all Naphtali, and the land of Ephraim, and Manasseh and all the land of Judah, unto the utmost sea.
>
> And the south, and the plain of the valley of Jericho, the city of palm trees, unto Zoar.
>
> And the Lord said unto him, This is the land which I sware unto Abraham, unto Isaac, and unto Jacob, saying, I will give it unto thy seed: I have caused thee to see it with thine eyes, but thou shalt not go thither.
>
> So Moses the servant of the Lord died there in the land of Moab, according to the word of the Lord.
>
> And he buried him in a valley in the land of Moab, over against Bethpeor, but no man knoweth his sepulchre unto this day.
>
> And Moses was a hundred and twenty years old when he died. His eye was not dim, nor his natural force abated.
>
> And the children of Israel wept for Moses in the plains of Moab thirty days: so the days of weeping and mourning for Moses were ended.

Here Toussaint stopped, and after a little period of silence began again but in a lower and less certain tone, a murmur unintelligible to me—perhaps it was a prayer. This was for all the world like a regular church service, though with the one man playing the roles of both priest and communicant.

I took my way toward my own berth, but sleep continues to elude me, though the hour is late. Therefore I write—to no one. The wind has risen and the seas run higher than they did at sunset, so that the lamp swings like a pendulum on its chain; it blots my page with shadow, and then once more returns its light. Though the ship is densely packed with men and I can hear my fellows snoring, I feel myself much alone this night.

Out of the groaning of the ship's timbers come again the words that Captain Savary repeated to a few of us at table: a sentence he claimed Toussaint had spoken when first taken onto the ship. *En me reversant, on n'a abattu à Saint-Domingue que le tronc de l'arbe de la liberté des noirs; il poussera par les racines, parce qu'elles sont profondes et nombreuses.* [In overthrowing me, you have done no more than cut the trunk of the tree of black liberty in Saint Domingue—it will spring back from the roots, for they are numerous and deep.]

Research Option

Using Research in Writing

Use the Internet, an encyclopedia, and books about Haiti to find out more about Toussaint L'Ouverture. Write a brief biographical sketch and share it with your classmates. Then discuss how your findings compare with the fictional portrait of Toussaint in this excerpt.

CHAPTER 8

Section 1

HISTORYMAKERS Simón Bolívar
The Liberator

"The bonds that united us to Spain have been severed."—Bolívar, **The Letter
from Jamaica** *(1814)*

Simón Bolívar led his people's fight for independence from Spain. He envisioned the formation of a single country extending from present-day Venezuela to modern Bolivia. However, his plans clashed with those of his followers, and the grand nation he dreamed of creating fell apart.

Bolívar was born in 1783 to a wealthy family from the colony of Venezuela. His education included several years of study in Europe. While there, he married, but soon after the couple reached South America his wife died of yellow fever.

Bolívar then returned to Europe and met with several important thinkers and politicians. One of them told Bolívar that the Spanish-American colonies had vast resources that could make them powerful— if only they could become free of Spanish control. Bolívar returned to South America and joined the movement for independence.

In 1810, a group of rebels in Venezuela removed the Spanish governor from office and took control. The next year Venezuela declared itself independent. By 1813, Bolívar commanded the army. In 1814, however, the Spanish fought back and defeated his troops, forcing him to flee the country.

During Bolívar's exile, he called for all Spanish colonies to rise against European rule to "avenge three centuries of shame." In 1814, he wrote a famous call to arms, *The Letter from Jamaica,* which outlined a plan to create republics reaching from Mexico to Argentina and Chile. Unable to win British or American support, he turned to Haiti. With money and guns from this newly independent republic, he returned to Venezuela to face the largest army Spain had ever sent across the Atlantic.

From 1815 to 1817, neither side won any decisive battles. However, Bolívar began to build the foundation of victory. He declared the end of slavery to be one of his goals, thus winning wider support. He made alliances with two groups of guerrilla soldiers, who harassed the Spanish army. He also hired veteran European troops. Then in 1819, he devised a daring plan to cross the Andes Mountains and surprise the Spanish. His army of 2,000 first had to cross the hot jungles of the Orinoco River

and then the freezing mountain passes. Many died, but Bolívar's army was strong enough to defeat the Spanish in four different battles.

Bolívar returned to the city of Angostura, Venezuela, and joined a congress working on forming the new government. With his urging, members voted to create the republic of Gran Colombia, which would include modern Colombia, Ecuador, and Venezuela. "The lessons of experience should not be lost on us," he said. Europe had too many countries that constantly fought each other. "A single government," he argued, "may use its great resources [to] lift us to the summit of power and prosperity." Bolívar was named president and military dictator of the new republic.

Bolívar won independence for Venezuela in 1821 and Ecuador in 1822. He freed Peru from Spain in 1824 and Upper Peru in 1825, which renamed itself Bolivia. He was president of Gran Colombia, Peru, and Bolivia. Bolívar hoped that these nations would unite and thus become stronger.

Others did not share this vision. Even Bolívar's closest allies in the fight for independence believed that there should be several countries, not one large one. By 1826, civil war had broken out. Two years later, Bolívar reacted to the crisis by declaring himself military dictator. Opponents attacked his palace and tried to assassinate him. The Liberator was now seen as an enemy of the state. Venezuela withdrew from Gran Colombia, and Ecuador followed. Finally, with his body wracked by tuberculosis and his heart sick over the conflict, Bolívar retired in 1830. He died later that year.

Questions

1. *Perceiving Relationships* Was Bolívar a better military or political leader? Explain.
2. *Organizing Facts and Details* What lesson did Bolívar draw from European history? What did he suggest doing in South America to prevent this problem?
3. *Making Judgments* Would you say that Bolívar was a success or a failure? Explain.

CHAPTER

8

Section 4

HISTORYMAKERS Ludwig van Beethoven
Innovative Genius

". . . My most prized possession, my hearing, has greatly deteriorated. . . . You will realize what a sad life I must now lead, . . . cut off from everything that is dear and precious to me."—Beethoven, letter to a friend (1801)

Ludwig van Beethoven was a towering genius whose struggles in life gave his music great power. Born into the classical tradition, he launched the romantic movement. Where vocal music had been thought the greatest achievement that music could reach, he made instrumental music supreme. He did all this despite being completely deaf for the last ten years of his life.

Beethoven's struggles began early. His family became steadily poorer when his grandfather died and his father became an alcoholic. Beethoven had to leave school, and by age 18 he was supporting his family. He was a talented piano player, and music became his career and his life. He studied for two months with another musical genius, Wolfgang Amadeus Mozart, who proclaimed "this young man will make a great name for himself in the world."

In 1792, at age 22, Beethoven left his home in Germany for Vienna, Austria. At the time, Vienna was the center of European music. There were many different professional groups, and the wealthy nobles were an eager audience. Beethoven played the piano at concerts. He also composed music, writing for both the piano and the orchestra. These early pieces were similar to the classical style of music then in fashion.

Around 1800, Beethoven found he was growing deaf. He played fewer concerts and spent more of his time writing music. Each year, he spent the warmer months in a rural village. He took walks in the country, stopping only to jot down a new musical idea. His notes show that he worked on some pieces for many years. Parts of his famous Fifth Symphony were first written in 1804, but the symphony was not completed until 1808.

Beethoven's music became extremely popular. Critics praised his work, and wealthy nobles paid Beethoven to dedicate a piece to them. Starting in 1808—and until his death in 1827—he received an annual salary from several nobles so that he could devote himself to writing. His life was without luxury, however, and visitors might have thought him poor. He never married, but after his death three letters that had never been sent were found addressed to a woman he called his "Immortal Beloved." Her identity has never been revealed.

In 1804, Beethoven launched a new style of music when he wrote his Third Symphony. It is called the *Eroica,* or heroic, symphony and was written on a grand scale. He dedicated the work to Napoleon. However, Beethoven, who supported republican government, removed the dedication in disgust after the French leader made himself emperor. Still, the piece reflects the great force of will that Napoleon brought to politics.

Beethoven produced many pieces, from piano music to string quartets to symphonies. His Sixth Symphony, called the *Pastoral,* was the first of a new kind of work called "program music." The composition was meant to tell a story. For example, light-hearted sections might suggest a pleasant day in the country, while darker, faster sounds might hint at a summer storm.

In his last 12 years, Beethoven hardly left his home at all. Complete deafness overtook him, and he could only communicate with friends by writing and reading notes. He wrote less music, but his new works were his most complex and moving yet. His crowning achievement was the Ninth Symphony, first performed in 1824. It combined an extra-large orchestra and a chorus, which ends the work by singing the stirring "Ode to Joy," a call for the fellowship of all people. At the performance, Beethoven turned the pages of the score for the conductor, keeping time with his foot. Unable to hear, he was unaware of the audience's enthusiastic applause.

Questions

1. *Recognizing Main Ideas* How did Beethoven suffer in his life?
2. *Making Inferences* How did Beethoven's work show the values of romanticism?
3. *Making Judgments* In what ways was Beethoven an innovator? Explain.

Name _____ Date _____

CONNECTIONS ACROSS TIME AND CULTURES

Bonds That Create a Nation-State

THEMATIC CONNECTION:
POWER AND AUTHORITY

As you learned in Chapter 24, nationalism led to the formation of nation-states. In a nation-state, people are linked by such common bonds as government, culture, and history. What common bonds do people in the United States today share? Work with a partner to fill in the chart below. If you need help, consult an almanac or encyclopedia.

Common Bonds That Link the People of the United States Today
1. Nationality:
2. Territory/Land:
3. Government:
4. Language:
5. Religion:
6. Culture:
7. Economy:
8. Other:

Name _____ Date _____

Determining Main Ideas The following questions deal with struggles against colonial rule in Latin America. Answer them in the space provided.

1. Describe the class system in Latin American countries.

   _____

   _____

2. What events and ideas helped bring about revolution in Latin America?

   _____

   _____

3. What was Simón Bolívar's role in the independence movement in the Spanish colonies?

   _____

   _____

4. How did Brazil achieve independence?

   _____

   _____

Reading Comprehension Find the name or term in the second column that best matches the description in the first column. Then write the letter of your answer in the blank.

_____ 5. Men who had been born in Spain and were at the top of Latin American society

_____ 6. Spaniards born in Latin America

_____ 7. Persons of mixed European and African ancestry

_____ 8. Persons of mixed European and Indian ancestry

_____ 9. Venezuelan-born liberator of Spanish colonies in Latin America

_____ 10. Priest who issued the *grito de Dolores*

a. Creoles

b. Padre Miguel Hidalgo

c. *peninsulares*

d. mestizos

e. Simón Bolívar

f. mulattos

CHAPTER

8

Section 2

RETEACHING ACTIVITY *Europe Faces Revolutions*

Summarizing Complete the chart below by summarizing information about the schools of political thought in Europe in the first half of the 1800s.

Schools of Political Thought	Details
Conservatives	1.
Liberals	2.
Radicals	3.

Reading Comprehension Find the name or term in the second column that best matches the description in the first column. Then write the letter of your answer in the blank.

_____ 4. The belief that one should be loyal not to a king or an empire but to a nation of people who share a culture and history

_____ 5. A nation with its own independent government

_____ 6. Region that includes all or part of present-day Greece, Albania, Bulgaria, Romania, Turkey, and the former Yugoslavia

_____ 7. Nephew of Napoleon Bonaparte who became emperor of France in 1852

_____ 8. Czar who moved Russia toward modernization and social change

a. the Balkans

b. Alexander II

c. nationalism

d. Louis-Napoleon

e. nation-state

CHAPTER
8
Section 3

RETEACHING ACTIVITY *Nationalism Case Study:*
Italy and Germany

Determining Main Ideas Write your answers in the blanks provided.

1. Powerful political idea of the 1800s that upset the balance of power in Europe:

   _____

2. Policy of forcing Russian culture on all ethnic groups in the Russian empire:

   _____

3. Sardinian prime minister who worked for Italian unification:

   _____

4. Leader of the Red Shirts who united the southern part of Italy with the Kingdom
   of Piedmont-Sardinia: _____

5. Very conservative members of Prussia's wealthy landowning class:

   _____

6. Prime minister under Wilhelm I: _____

7. Term applied to tough power politics with no room for idealism:

   _____

8. War between Austria and Prussia in 1866: _____

9. War between Prussia and France that was the final stage in German unification:

   _____

10. Title taken by King Wilhelm of Prussia during the Second Reich:

    _____

CHAPTER
8
Section 4

RETEACHING ACTIVITY *Revolutions in the Arts*

Reading Comprehension Find the name or term in the second column that best matches the description in the first column. Then write the letter of your answer in the blank.

_____ 1. Arts movement that had a deep interest in nature and the individual

_____ 2. Freedom-fighter in Greece and leading romantic poet

_____ 3. Great German romantic writer

_____ 4. Collected German fairy tales and created a dictionary and grammar of the German language

_____ 5. French romantic who wrote *The Hunchback of Notre Dame*

_____ 6. Wrote the early successful Gothic horror novel *Frankenstein*

_____ 7. Greatest romantic composer

_____ 8. Innovation that became a tool for scientific investigation and led to the development of motion pictures

_____ 9. Movement in art that reflected the growing political importance of the working class in the 1850s

_____10. Term for the first practical photographs

_____11. Famous English realist novelist who wrote about London's working poor

_____12. Type of art that attempted to give the artist's impression of a subject or moment in time

A. Goethe

B. photography

C. romanticism

D. impressionism

E. Beethoven

F. Victor Hugo

G. realism

H. Charles Dickens

I. the Grimm brothers

J. daguerreotypes

K. Byron

L. Mary Shelley

Answer Key

Chapter 5, Section 1
GUIDED READING

A. Possible responses:

1. Spain built a powerful army and navy, and its monarchs and nobles became patrons of artists, leading to a golden age in the arts.

2. As the population grew, people demanded more food and other goods, so merchants were able to raise prices. As silver bullion flooded the market, its value dropped and it took more to buy anything.

3. severe inflation, lack of a middle class, expulsion of Jews and Muslims, outdated manufacturing methods, and the high cost of wars

4. The Dutch rebelled and eventually the largely Protestant northern provinces of the Netherlands united and declared independence from Spain.

5. stable government, strong middle class, large naval fleet, mighty trading empire

6. decline of feudalism, rise of cities, creation of a middle class, and growth of national kingdoms

B. Possible response: Philip II was a forceful ruler in many ways. He tried to control every aspect of his empire's affairs and believed that all power in his state rested in his hands.

Chapter 5, Section 3
GUIDED READING

A. Possible responses:

1. converted to Catholicism and issued Edict of Nantes, which declared that Huguenots could live in peace in France and set up their own houses of worship in certain cities; devoted his reign to rebuilding France and its prosperity

2. forbade Protestant cities from having walls; weakened power of nobles by ordering them to take down their fortified castles and by increasing power of government agents

3. turned them to skepticism, the idea that nothing can be known for certain, and led them to question church doctrine, which claimed to be the only truth

4. followed a strict policy of mercantilism by taking steps to make France self-sufficient, expanding and protecting French industries, and encouraging migration to France's colony of Canada, where the fur trade would add to French commercial strength

5. popularized opera and ballet, supported writers such as Molière, promoted art that glorified the monarchy and supported absolute rule

6. His many enemies combined forces in the League of Augsburg and thereby became strong enough to stop France.

7. made France a power in Europe and a model of culture, but laid the groundwork for revolution because of staggering debts and royal abuse of power

B. Possible responses:

Skepticism is the belief that there can never be absolute knowledge of what is true.

Intendants were French government agents who collected taxes and administered justice; Louis XIV used them to keep power under his central authority.

Chapter 5, Section 3
GUIDED READING

A. Possible responses:

1. Responses may cite the tension between Catholic and Lutheran princes in Germany, their fear of the spread of Calvinism, and Ferdinand's attempt to limit Protestantism and then to crush a Protestant revolt in Bohemia.

2. Responses may mention that it devastated Germany so that it did not become a unified state until the 1800s; weakened the Hapsburg states of Spain and Austria; strengthened France, which received German territory; ended religious wars in Europe; and marked the beginning of the modern state system.

3. The economy of western Europe was commercial and capitalistic while that of central Europe remained feudal, dependent on serf labor, and untouched by the commercial revolution.

4. Strong landowning nobles hindered the development of strong monarchy. The Thirty Years' War had weakened the Holy Roman Empire.

5. Responses may mention that during the Thirty Years' War, they reconquered Bohemia, wiped out Protestantism there, and created a loyal Czech nobility. After the war, they centralized the government and created a standing army.

6. Responses may mention that they created a strong standing army; created a military state and bought the loyalty of the Junkers by giving the landowning nobility the exclusive right to be officers in the army; weakened representative assemblies; and took over Silesia.

B. Possible response: Maria Theresa was a decisive and ambitious ruler, as evidenced by her success in stopping Prussia's aggression and in allying with a former enemy to stop an even stronger foe. Frederick II was a strong and aggressive leader in foreign affairs but compassionate in domestic affairs.

Chapter 5, Section 4
GUIDED READING

A. Possible responses:

1. increased powers as absolute ruler

2. replaced patriarch with Holy Synod to run Church under his direction

3. recruited able men from lower-ranking families, gave them positions of authority, and rewarded them with land grants, making them loyal to him alone

4. expanded army and hired European officers to train soldiers who served for life; imposed heavy taxes to pay for his huge, improved army

5. introduced potatoes, which became staple of Russian diet; started first Russian newspaper; ordered nobles to adopt Western fashions; raised status of women by having them attend social gatherings; advanced education by opening schools and ordering some to leave Russia to study

6. went to war against Sweden to gain a port on the Baltic Coast

7. forced thousands of serfs to work on building St. Petersburg on unhealthy swampy land

8. ordered many Russian nobles to leave Moscow and settle in the new port city capital

B. Possible response: Ivan IV crowned himself czar and ruled justly from 1547 to 1560. He became known as Ivan the Terrible because he set up a police state and killed his eldest son in a violent quarrel.

Chapter 5, Section 5
GUIDED READING

A. Possible responses:

1. struggled with Parliament over money; offended Puritan members of Parliament by refusing to make Puritan reforms

2. Struggles over money led to forced signing of Petition of Right, dissolution of Parliament, passage of laws limiting royal power, effort to arrest leaders of Parliament, and finally the English Civil War.

3. Cromwell abolished the monarchy and the House of Lords; later he sent the remaining members of Parliament home and ruled as a dictator.

4. Parliament invited Charles II to rule and passed *habeas corpus,* which limited king's power to jail opponents.

5. fought over appointment of Catholics to high office in violation of English law

6. governed as partners, with power of monarchy limited by Bill of Rights

B. Possible responses:

Restoration: period when the monarchy was restored after collapse of Puritan government

Habeas corpus: 1679 law that gave every prisoner the right to obtain a document ordering that the prisoner be brought before a judge to specify charges against the prisoner

Glorious Revolution: bloodless overthrow of Catholic King James II in favor of Protestant William and Mary

Cabinet: government ministers who became link between monarch and Parliament

Constitutional monarch: a king or queen who rules with power limited by law

Chapter 5
BUILDING VOCABULARY

A. Multiple Choice

1. b
2. a
3. c

4. b
5. c
6. b

B. Evaluating

1. F; Maria Teresa was the ruler of Austria and Frederick the Great was the ruler of Prussia during the Seven Years' War, in which the great European powers fought one another on three continents.

2. T

3. F; The rule of Charles II in England is known as the Restoration because the monarchy was brought back.

C. Writing

Possible Answer

After 1688, England became a constitutional monarchy. In this form of government, the power of a king or queen is limited by laws. This change went against the trend in Europe, where rulers had been increasing their powers and ruling as absolute monarchs. An absolute monarch holds all the power within his or her country. Absolute monarchies were supported by the idea of divine right, meaning that the monarch is God's representative on earth.

Chapter 5, Section 4
SKILLBUILDER PRACTICE

Possible responses:

1. Short-term effects were a more modern look for Russian nobles and tension between the czar and the boyars.

2. Long-term effects were reform in Russia and an ongoing debate and resentment over acceptance of foreign ideas.

3. The symbolism was that he was "cutting off" old ways—getting rid of tradition.

4. Answers will vary. The decision showed that Peter was determined to reform Russia although he had to force change on his people. It angered the Russians and intensified their fear of change.

Chapter 5, Section 3
GEOGRAPHY APPLICATION

Responses may vary on the inferential questions. Sample responses are given for those.

1. Austrian Empire

2. Ottoman Empire and the Holy Roman Empire; the Ottoman Empire decreases by about 700 miles; the Holy Roman Empire decreases by 150 miles

3. Prussia, Russia, Austria

4. It was located in south-central Europe. It was not in the middle of these new empires, but located on the southern edge.

5. approximately 150 miles; approximately 600 miles

6. These old empires had a weak central government, an inefficient administration, and too much diversity of people.

7. These new states had a strong central monarch, a standing army, and a professional civil service and administration.

Chapter 5, Section 2
PRIMARY SOURCE

Louis XIV's Advice to His Son

1. Informally assess students' role-playing to make sure they understand the king's perspective on being a ruler.

2. Lists will vary but should include the following: have government officials consult with the king, keep track of finances, have subjects make requests directly, do not have a prime minister, assign duties carefully, choose ministers wisely. Guide students to understand that Louis XIV ruled absolutely, whereas his father appointed a strong minister—Cardinal Richelieu—who ruled France.

Chapter 5, Section 4
PRIMARY SOURCE

Peter the Great's Reforms

Possible responses:

1. January 1, 1700; by praying; decorating streets and homes with trees, pine, and fir branches; firing guns; and displaying fireworks

2. They would not be allowed to marry.

3. Possible advantages: bridged the gap between Russia and Europe, helped Russia compete economically and socially. Possible disadvantages: caused disquieting changes in daily life, created resentment among those Russian citizens who held onto cultural traditions, increased Peter the Great's power as absolute monarch.

Chapter 5, Section 5
PRIMARY SOURCE

Diary of Samuel Pepys

1. Charts will vary but should include the following effects: many houses, churches, and other buildings were burned; families were forced to flee their homes; pigeons died; and the city was blanketed by smoke and cinders. You may want to encourage students to do further research about the fire and add more effects to their charts.

2. Before students begin, provide them with copies of several different newspapers. Point out how lead paragraphs are typically written. Then informally assess students' paragraphs. You may want to extend this activity by having students use information in this excerpt to write full news stories about the fire.

Chapter 5, Section 5
PRIMARY SOURCE

English Bill of Rights

Students' diagrams will vary but should include the following. Similarities: both sought to protect individual liberties such as freedom of speech and to limit the powers of the government. Differences: the English Bill of Rights addresses issues related to the king versus Parliamentary authority.

Chapter 5, Section 2
LITERATURE SELECTION

The Cat and the King

Possible responses:

1. two factions of the king's court, the "Lorrainers" and their wives and the rest of the French dukes and their wives

2. He improved his reputation at court and gained an apartment in Versailles.

3. The king controlled the nobles completely, and nobles did whatever they thought would please the king in order to improve their status at court.

Chapter 5, Section 3
HISTORYMAKERS

Maria Theresa

Possible responses:

1. The main idea is that Maria Theresa was a determined queen who wanted to protect her country, strengthen her control over it, and help her people.

2. She was a determined person with a strong will, as shown by her decision to fight for Silesia even though her advisers told her to give it up.

3. She was a good queen because the orders she issued resulted in many benefits—such as lower taxes and the creation of public education—for her people.

Chapter 5, Section 5
HISTORYMAKERS

William of Orange

Possible responses:

1. The Protestant religion was probably more important to William. This is shown in his quest to curb the power of Catholic France throughout his life. Also, because he was born and raised in the Netherlands, the idea of "English liberties" probably did not mean as much to him.

2. The English turned to William first because he had a claim on the throne, both by himself and with Mary, and second because he was a powerful Protestant figure.

3. Succession refers to the plan for inheriting a throne. It was significant in this period because it was thought that the ruler would impose his religion on the nation.

Chapter 5, Section 4
CONNECTIONS ACROSS TIME AND CULTURES

Possible responses:

1. Absolute monarchs believed in divine right—God created the monarchy and an absolute monarch responded only to God.

2. They made the nobles dependent on them and used land grants and government appointments to gain the support of the middle class.

3. To enhance their prestige, European rulers tried to weaken the power of the Church and started wars to settle religious conflicts.

4. Peasants had no rights or freedoms and existed to serve the state.

5. Many became patrons of the arts, constructed transportation networks, built standing armies and navies, and fought wars.

6. territorial conflicts, war, widespread rebellion and social unrest, economic decline

Chapter 5, Section 1
RETEACHING ACTIVITY

1. a. Charles inherited Spain and its American colonies, and parts of Italy, Austria, and the Netherlands.

   b. When Charles retired to a monastery, he divided his empire between his brother, Ferdinand, and his son, Philip II.

2. a. He seized the Portuguese kingdom, which gave him an empire that circled the globe.

   b. With the wealth from this empire, Spain was able to build a large standing army.

3. a. In 1571, the pope called on Catholic rulers to attack the Ottoman Empire. Philip sent a large Spanish fleet, which defeated an Ottoman Fleet near Lepanto.

   b. In 1588, the Spanish Armada was defeated in an attack on Protestant England.

4. a. El Greco and Velázquez were two of the most important painters of the period.

   b. Cervantes' book, *Don Quixote de la Mancha,* published in 1605, is sometimes thought of as the first modern European novel.

5. a. Severe inflation was partly the result of population growth.

   b. Spain never developed a middle class because the tax burden was on the lower classes.

6. a. The guilds made Spanish goods more expensive than imported

goods, so Spain used its great wealth to buy goods from foreigners.

b. Most of those foreigners were Spain's enemies.

7. a. The Dutch in the Spanish Netherlands were involved in trade and had a thriving middle class.

b. Philip tried to crush Protestantism in the Netherlands, but after an 11-year fight, seven northern provinces declared themselves independent of Spain and took the name United Provinces of the Netherlands.

Chapter 5, Section 2
RETEACHING ACTIVITY

1. M
2. E
3. J
4. B
5. A
6. L
7. G
8. I
9. C
10. K
11. D
12. F

Chapter 5, Section 3
RETEACHING ACTIVITY

1. 1618
2. Catholicism and Protestantism
3. Ferdinand II
4. by being allowed to rob German villages
5. Gustavus Adolphus and his army
6. because they feared the Hapsburgs more than the Protestants
7. She decreased their power.
8. Hapsburgs; Austria
9. Prussia
10. He felt a ruler should be like a father to his people.
11. Maria Theresa forged an alliance with France that brought it into the war.
12. Britain, because it gained sole economic domination of India

Chapter 5, Section 4
RETEACHING ACTIVITY

1. a
2. d
3. c
4. a
5. b
6. b
7. d
8. c

Chapter 5, Section 5
RETEACHING ACTIVITY

1. James I
2. Parliament
3. Charles I
4. English Civil War
5. Oliver Cromwell
6. Restoration
7. *habeas corpus*
8. Whigs, Tories
9. James I
10. constitutional monarchy
11. cabinet
12. prime minister

Chapter 6, Section 1
GUIDED READING

A. Possible responses:

1. Renaissance inspired spirit of curiosity; discoveries of classical manuscripts led to realization that ancient scholars often did not agree; scholars began to question ideas that had been accepted for hundreds of years; printing press spread new ideas quickly.

2. Long sea voyages required better navigational instruments, which led to research in astronomy and mathematics. As scientists looked more closely at the world around them, they made discoveries that did not match ancient beliefs.

3. Planets revolve around the sun.

4. Mathematical laws govern planetary motion; orbits of the planets are elliptical, not circular.

5. Each pendulum swing takes the same amount of time; falling objects accelerate at a fixed rate; Jupiter has moons.

6. The same force—gravity—rules all matter on earth and in space. Every object in the universe attracts every other; the degree of attraction is determined by mass and distance.

7. invention of telescope, microscope, barometer, thermometer

8. study of human anatomy, first vaccine (against smallpox)

9. Boyle's law explaining relationship of volume, temperature, and pressure of gas; discovery of oxygen

B. Possible response: The scientific method, which uses observation, experimentation, and reasoning to reach new conclusions, is based on Bacon's empirical, or experimental, method and on Descartes's belief that mathematics and logic should be the means to arrive at and express basic truths about the natural world.

Chapter 6, Section 2
GUIDED READING

A. Possible responses:

1. believed in tolerance, reason, and freedom of thought, expression, and religious belief; fought against prejudice and superstition

2. advocated separation of powers and checks and balances to keep any individual or group from gaining complete control of government

3. committed to individual freedom; viewed government as an agreement among free individuals to create a society guided by the "general will"; unlike other Enlightenment thinkers, believed that civilization corrupted people's natural goodness and destroyed freedom and equality

4. believed laws existed to preserve social order; advocated a criminal justice system based on fairness and reason

5. believed that women, like men, need education to become virtuous and useful; argued for women's rights to become educated and to participate in politics

B. Possible response: encouraged people to judge for themselves what was right or wrong in society and to rely on human reason to solve social problems

C. Possible response: In Hobbes's view, because people always acted in their own self-interest, they needed a social contract, or government, to keep order; the best government would be an absolute monarchy that could impose order and demand obedience. Locke believed people were reasonable beings with the natural ability to govern themselves. The purpose of government was to protect their natural rights of life, liberty, and property.

Chapter 6, Section 3
GUIDED READING

A. Possible responses:

1. spread enlightened thinking in all areas by publishing the *Encyclopedia*

2. broke from traditionally ornate musical forms and developed the sonata and symphony

3. set a new standard for elegance and originality with his varied and numerous musical compositions

4. exhibited great range in his works; moved from the classical style of Mozart to begin new trend that carried music into the Age of Romanticism

5. wrote *Pamela*, the first English novel

6. committed himself to the goal of reforming and strengthening his country; granted many religious freedoms, reduced censorship, improved education and the justice system, and abolished torture; considered that the king should be "first servant of the state"

7. abolished serfdom, initiated legal reforms, introduced freedom of the press, supported freedom of religion

8. tried to modernize and reform Russia according to the writings of the philosophes; accomplished limited reforms

B. Possible responses:

Salon: social gathering in a person's home at which enlightened thinkers shared ideas and enjoyed artistic performances

Baroque: grand ornate style of the arts that was popular before the Enlightenment

Neoclassical: simple and elegant style of the arts that emphasized order and balance and borrowed ideas and themes from classical Greece and Rome

Enlightened despot: absolute monarch who reflected Enlightenment ideals of reform and reason

Chapter 6, Section 4
GUIDED READING

A. Possible responses:

1. Cause: need to pay off debts from French and Indian War

   Effect: Colonists boycott British manufactured goods in protest; Parliament repeals Stamp Act tax.

2. Cause: Colonists protest an import tax on tea and dump tea off British ships.

   Effect: First Continental Congress meets to protest punishment of Boston.

3. Cause: British soldiers and American militiamen exchange fire at Lexington and Concord.

   Effect: American Revolution begins.

4. Cause: France wants to weaken its enemy Britain.

   Effect: Combined forces result in victory for the Americans.

5. Cause: States need a plan for a national government but want to protect their own authority.

   Effect: National government is set up but is powerless to govern.

B. Possible response: The Declaration of Independence uses the political ideas of John Locke to defend rebellion against a government that abuses the natural rights of its people. The U.S. Constitution, with its system of checks and balances and federal system dividing powers between national and state governments, reflects Montesquieu's ideas of separation and balance of powers. The Bill of Rights guarantees many of the rights and freedoms advocated by the philosophers, such as freedom of speech, freedom of religion, and protecting the rights of people who are accused of crimes.

Chapter 6
BUILDING VOCABULARY

A. Matching

1. c
2. e
3. h
4. b
5. a
6. g
7. f

8. d

B. Completion

1. neoclassical
2. federal system
3. Declaration of Independence
4. Bill of Rights
5. salons
6. social contract

C. Writing

Possible Answer

Before 1500, most scholars referred to ancient Greek and Roman texts or to the Bible to determine what was true about the physical world. They believed in Aristotle's geocentric theory, which stated that the earth was the center of the universe and all the heavenly bodies revolved around the earth. But in the 1500s, the Polish astronomer Nicolaus Copernicus challenged this theory. Based on his observations, Copernicus proposed a heliocentric theory, stating that the sun was the center of the universe and the stars and planets revolved around the sun. Copernicus and other scientists of the 1500s and 1600s began a revolution in scientific thinking known as the Scientific Revolution. Scientific thinking became based on careful observation and questioning of accepted beliefs. As a result of the Scientific Revolution, a new approached to science developed. Called the scientific method, it provides a logical procedure for gathering and testing ideas.

Chapter 6, Section 1
SKILLBUILDER PRACTICE

Possible responses:

1. Physicist: a scientist who studies matter, energy, and the interaction between the two; dynamics: study of the relationship between motion and the forces affecting motion; oscillation: swing from one side to the other

2. Galileo made many important discoveries in the field of physics.

3. Galileo founded the science of dynamics with his discoveries of the law of the pendulum and the acceleration of falling objects at predictable rates. His law of the pendulum led to a more accurate way to measure time.

Chapter 22 Section 1
GEOGRAPHY APPLICATION

Responses may vary on the inferential questions. Sample responses are given for those.

1. Earth
2. Sun
3. Mars
4. the moon
5. It was the fourth most distant heavenly body, with only Mars being more distant.
6. Venus and Mercury
7. Copernicus believed that the planets revolved around the sun in perfect circles, while Kepler believed they move around in ellipses.
8. Ptolemy used unscientific observation, while Kepler proved his theories with mathematics.

   Most students will indicate that Ptolemy's method would not be acceptable today. They may note that people today demand more than simple observation.

Chapter 6, Section 1
PRIMARY SOURCE

Starry Messenger

Informally assess students' participation in researching, planning, and creating the bulletin board display.

Chapter 6, Section 2
PRIMARY SOURCE

The Social Contract

Possible responses:

1. a government freely formed by the people
2. No; he believed that being strong and forceful did not necessarily give the strongest the right to rule unless the people willed it.
3. Both Locke and Rousseau believed that legitimate government came from the consent of the governed.

Chapter 6, Section 2
PRIMARY SOURCE

Two Treatises on Government

1. Informally assess students' definitions. Help them to understand the difference between Locke's concept of natural liberty and liberty in society.
2. Before students begin this activity, remind them that Filmer supported the idea of absolute monarchy and the divine right of kings while Locke believed that the power of government came from the consent of the people. Then informally assess students' role-playing.

Chapter 6, Section 2
PRIMARY SOURCE

A Vindication of the Rights of Woman

Possible responses:

1. She believed that being denied the chance to fully develop their abilities and talents made women weak and wretched.
2. In her opinion, women were physically inferior but, like men, needed education to become virtuous and useful.
3. Some students may say that she might have agreed with him because she felt that education helped women become "affectionate wives and rational mothers." Others may say that she might have disagreed with him because she stressed that the purpose of education was to help women develop their talents and abilities and, in turn, make them more noble.

Chapter 6, Section 4
PRIMARY SOURCE

The Declaration of Independence

Possible responses:

1. to tell the world why the colonies have decided to separate from Britain
2. to secure the "unalienable" rights of the people—life, liberty, and the pursuit of happiness; when a government destroys the unalienable rights of people
3. Jefferson probably felt that one despotism breeds another, that people have an obligation to end tyranny and to

preserve liberty in much the same way as they have an obligation to stop crime and evil. In this sense, it is a moral obligation.

Chapter 6, Section 1
LITERATURE SELECTION

The Recantation of Galileo Galilei

1. Informally assess students' interpretations of the characters. Students may prefer to perform a Reader's Theater version of the excerpt.
2. Informally assess students' participation in the discussion. Guide them to understand that if Galileo confesses he will act in a manner contrary to the scientific method on which he has based his career; on the other hand, if he does not confess, he will be executed.
3. Informally assess students' playbills on the basis of creativity and on how effectively they reflect the content of the play.

Chapter 6, Section 1
HISTORYMAKERS

Nicolaus Copernicus

Possible responses:

1. He used his observations to conclude that the earth rotated on its axis, moved around the sun, and moved up and down on its axis.
2. Copernicus's theory was accepted even though it was not perfect because it offered an answer to the question of the location of Venus and Mercury. Also, he had better and simpler explanations of the movement of the planets.
3. His explanation that every object tended toward a different center helped his theory because it explained why everything on earth did not fall to the sun, which, he said, was the center of the solar system.

Chapter 6, Section 2
HISTORYMAKERS

Baron de Montesquieu

Possible responses:

1. Montesquieu was wealthy. His estates, his wife's fortunes, and the sale of his

judgeship allowed him to travel widely and spend his time reading and writing.

2. Montesquieu thought that without limits, a single power could become dangerous.

3. Montesquieu was more conservative than other writers of the Enlightenment. He did not believe in government by the people and was willing to protect the privileges enjoyed by nobles.

Chapter 6, Section 1
CONNECTIONS ACROSS TIME AND CULTURES

1. Standards of order, balance, and proportion are reflected in the neoclassical style of art and architecture.

2. Both Greek dramatists and Enlightenment novelists wrote fiction with carefully crafted plots and thought-provoking characters. While Greek tragedies usually tell stories of important people, Enlightenment novels often focus on the experiences of common people. Voltaire, like the comic satirists of ancient Greece, became famous for his satires critical of government, politics, and the aristocracy.

3. Both believed in the discovery of truth and understanding of natural laws through reason and logic.

4. The scientific method, like the method used by Aristotle, uses reason and logic, in addition to experimentation and observation, to test ideas about the nature of the universe.

5. In both periods, traditional values and accepted beliefs were questioned and there was a surge in intellectual and artistic activity.

6. Answers might include establishing the scientific method, thinking about ways to organize government, and believing in the importance of the individual in society.

Chapter 6, Section 1
RETEACHING ACTIVITY

1. geocentric theory: believed that God established the earth as a fixed object in the center of the universe, and that the moon, sun, and stars all moved in circular paths around the earth; heliocentric theory: believed that the stars, the earth, and the other planets all revolved around the sun

2. One factor was the extensive European exploration taking place. It made people open to new ideas and questions. Another was the invention of the printing press, which helped to spread new ideas.

3. Galileo's work in astronomy contradicted Church positions on the nature of the universe and earth's role in it. The pope had Galileo tried by the Inquisition, and Galileo was forced to deny the truth of his ideas.

4. first microscope invented by Zacharias Janssen; the first mercury barometer invented by Evangelista Torrecelli; first thermometer to use mercury in glass invented by Gabriel Fahrenheit

5. d

6. a

7. f

8. b

9. c

10. e

Chapter 6, Section 2
RETEACHING ACTIVITY

1. b

2. d

3. a

4. b

5. c

6. d

7. a

8. c

Chapter 6, Section 3
RETEACHING ACTIVITY

1. Diderot began to pubish a series of books in 1751 that were compilations of articles from leading scholars. Even though the French government and the Catholic Church censored the *Encyclopedia,* it was responsible for spreading Enlightenment ideas all over Europe.

2. Neoclassical art began to replace baroque art during the late 1700s. Neoclassical art followed a simple and elegant style that drew on ideas from classical Greece and Rome.

3. Classical music, with a new, lighter style, emerged during the Enlightenment. Haydn, Mozart, and Beethoven were three classical composers from Austria.

4. Eighteenth century writers began writing novels, lengthy works of prose fiction. *Pamela,* by Samuel Richardson, is often considered the first English novel.

5. Enlightened despots supported the ideas of the philosophes and made enlightenment reforms. Europe's most important enlightened despots included Frederick II of Prussia, Joseph II of Austria, and Catherine the Great of Russia.

6. Ruled Prussia from 1740 to 1786; granted religious freedoms, reduced censorship, improved education

7. Ruled Russia from 1762 to 1796; put in place limited reforms; vastly enlarged the Russian empire

Chapter 6, Section 4
RETEACHING ACTIVITY

1. F; The trade law called the Navigation Act prevented American colonists from selling their goods to any country other than Britain.

2. F; The French and Indian War was fought between France and England for control of the North American continent.

3. T

4. T

5. F; The Boston Tea Party was the name given to the dumping of tea into Boston Harbor to protest British taxes on its import.

6. T

7. F; Thomas Jefferson was the author of the Declaration of Independence.

8. T

9. F; The French entered the war on the side of the American colonists in 1778.

10. T

Chapter 7, Section 1
GUIDED READING

A. Possible responses:

1. The First Estate and Second Estate had privileges not granted to the Third Estate, to which about 97 percent of the people belonged. Heavily taxed

and discontented, the Third Estate was eager for change.

2. People of the Third Estate began questioning long-standing ideas about government and spoke of equality and liberty.

3. A heavy tax burden, high prices, food shortages, and extravagant spending by the king and queen fueled discontent.

4. An indecisive king put off dealing with the crisis until it was too late.

5. Delegates of the Third Estate refused to be dominated by the clergy and nobles and asserted their independence.

6. It marked the end of absolute monarchy and the beginning of representative government.

7. In response, the king yielded to the demands of the National Assembly.

8. The fall of the Bastille into the control of French common people became a symbolic act of revolution.

B. Possible response: Rumors of outlaws terrorizing peasants, revenge for feudal laws, and rising bread prices combined to cause senseless panic and fear to sweep France.

Chapter 7, Section 2
GUIDED READING

A. Possible responses:

1. liberty, property, security, resistance to oppression, equal justice, freedom of speech, freedom of religion

2. Many were conservative Catholics who were offended by attempts to make the church a part of the state.

3. radicals, moderates, conservatives

4. that the revolution would spread beyond France and affect their countries

5. The Legislative Assembly gave up the idea of a limited monarchy, deposed the king, and called for the election of a new legislature to replace itself.

6. to build a "republic of virtue"

7. People of all classes grew weary of the Terror and shifted from radical left to conservative right.

B. Possible responses:

Émigrés: nobles on extreme right who wanted to restore Old Regime

sans-culottes: wage-earners and shop-keepers on extreme left who wanted a greater voice in government

Jacobins: members of a radical political organization

Chapter 7, Section 3
GUIDED READING

A. Possible responses:

1. Goal(s): Stable economy and more equality in taxation

   Result(s): Steady supply of tax money, better control of economy, financial management

2. Goal(s): Comprehensive and uniform system of laws

   Result(s): Elimination of many injustices; promotion of order over individual rights, which were restricted

3. Goal(s): Regaining French control; restoring productive sugar industry

   Result(s): Failure; death of thousands of soldiers

4. Goal(s): Make money; cut losses in Americas; punish British

   Result(s): Assured power of U.S.; gave England a powerful rival

5. Goal(s): Remove threat of British navy; defeat major enemy

   Result(s): Assured supremacy of British navy; forced Napoleon to give up plans to invade Britain

B. Possible response: In November 1799, in a coup d'état, Napoleon overthrew the Directory and assumed dictatorial powers as the first consul of the French republic. In 1800, a plebiscite approved a new constitution that gave all real power to Napoleon as first consul.

Chapter 7, Section 4
GUIDED READING

A. Possible responses:

1. It weakened economies of France and other lands under Napoleon's control more than it damaged Britain.

2. Loss of many soldiers weakened French Empire; enflamed nationalistic feelings encouraged conquered peoples to turn against French.

3. Desperate French soldiers deserted in search of food because of Russian scorched-earth policy.

4. Unable to advance further, French soldiers retreated; all but 10,000 died of exhaustion, hunger, and the cold.

5. Coalition defeated inexperienced French army; Napoleon's empire crumbled.

6. European armies defeated French forces and ended Napoleon's last bid for power.

B. Possible response: For what is called the Hundred Days, Napoleon ruled again as emperor of France until he was defeated in battle near Waterloo and exiled to St. Helena.

Chapter 7, Section 5
GUIDED READING

A. Possible responses:

Members and Representatives: Five European "great powers"—Austria, Prussia, and Russia represented by their rulers and Britain and France by their foreign ministers

Goals: Establish lasting peace and stability in Europe; prevent future French aggression; restore balance of power; restore royal families to thrones

Actions Taken: Formed Kingdom of the Netherlands; created German Confederation; recognized independence of Switzerland; added Genoa to Kingdom of Sardinia; required France to return territories conquered by Napoleon but left France a major power; affirmed principle of legitimacy

Legacy: Short-term: Conservatives regained control of governments; triggered revolts in colonies

Long-term: Created an age of peace in Europe; diminished power of France and increased power of Britain and Prussia; sparked growth of nationalism

B. Possible response: Metternich sought to maintain peace between European nations by creating a balance of power among rival countries so no country would be a threat to the others. To guard against revolutions, he set up a series of alliances called the Concert of Europe, which required nations to help one another if a revolution erupted.

Chapter 7
BUILDING VOCABULARY

A. Matching

1. g
2. e
3. f
4. h
5. c
6. b
7. d
8. a

B. Completion

1. Marie Antoinette
2. Tennis Court Oath
3. National Assembly
4. Maximilien Robespierre
5. Klemens von Metternich
6. Continental System

C. Writing

Possible Answer

Napoleon Bonaparte was a general in the French army when he staged a coup d'etat, or sudden seizure of power, in 1799 and made himself dictator of France. As a successful general and able administrator, he became a popular leader. He thought his greatest achievement was a uniform set of laws called the Napoleonic Code, which promoted law and order over individual rights. Through military conquests, Napoleon built up a large French empire. However, he suffered a major defeat in the Battle of Trafalgar in 1805. In this naval battle, the British destroyed the French fleet. Napoleon's continued efforts to defeat the British contributed to his downfall. The main powers of Europe joined forces against him and drove him from power. Although he regained power, Napoleon was defeated for the final time at the village of Waterloo in Belgium in 1815.

Chapter 7, Section 4
SKILLBUILDER PRACTICE

Possible responses:

1. Any three of the following: Spain, the Kingdom of Naples, northeastern Italy, Switzerland, the Confederation of the Rhine, the Grand Duchy of Warsaw

2. The distance from northwest Spain to the eastern border of the Grand Duchy of Warsaw is about 1,700 miles.

3. northwest

4. The southern tip of Spain at the Strait of Gibraltar

5. Sweden, the Kingdom of Denmark and Norway, the United Kingdom of Great Britain and Ireland, Portugal, Sardinia, Sicily, and the Ottoman Empire

6. The area of the lands controlled by Napoleon is much larger than the combined areas of European countries that were not allied with Napoleon or controlled by him.

7. about 1,600 miles

8. Any three of the following: Trafalgar, Ulm, Jena, Austerlitz, Wagram, Friedland, Aspern, La Coruna, Talavera, Madrid, and Valencia

Chapter 7, Section 2
GEOGRAPHY APPLICATION

Responses may vary on the inferential questions. Sample responses are given for those.

1. Spain; Austria and Prussia

2. the northeast

3. two; east of Paris and northeast of Paris in the annexed area of the Austrian Netherlands

4. They are all cities located in areas of France where the Revolution was resisted by royalists and conservative peasants.

5. Britain sent émigré troops by ship to support French regions in the west and the south of France that resisted the Revolution.

6. Austrian and Prussian troops moved from the Austrian Netherlands toward Paris, winning a battle along the way. At Valmy, just east of Paris, however, the foreign troops were defeated. This marked the turning point of the war.

Chapter 7, Section 2
PRIMARY SOURCE

A Declaration of the Rights of Man and of the Citizen

1. Through their research, students will find that Marie Joseph de Lafayette wrote the declaration using the Virginia Declaration of Rights as a model. Encourage students to find and share additional information about the declaration.

2. Charts will vary but should indicate that all three defined the rights of citizens. Both the French and English documents guaranteed citizens' rights by law. While the American document declared the colonies' independence from Britain and outlined the powers of independent states, the English document created a limited monarchy.

3. Article 1 condemns needless social distinctions, such as the division of society into the three estates. Several other articles, including articles 2, 4, and 5, also emphasize the equality of all, regardless of class. Article 13 forbids a tax system in which nobles pay nothing and the Third Estate pays about half of its earnings in taxes.

Chapter 7, Section 2
PRIMARY SOURCE

La Marseillaise

1. Informally assess students' participation in the class discussion. You may wish to have students write their responses down.

2. Informally assess students' role-playing.

3. Informally assess students' comparisons. As an alternative, you may want to have them create a Venn diagram to compare the music, lyrics, and historical circumstances of the two anthems.

Chapter 7, Section 2
PRIMARY SOURCE

The Execution of Louis XVI

Possible responses:

1. He responded in a calm, proud, dignified, courageous, and defiant manner.

2. At first they responded silently, but then they cried "Vive la République!" and threw their hats in the air in celebration.

3. Students should realize that the drums would keep the crowd from hearing the king's words, which might stir sympathy for him. Remind students that the drums mentioned in the second paragraph of the selection were to drown out expressions in favor of the king.

Chapter 7, Section 3
PRIMARY SOURCE

Napoleon's Proclamation at Austerlitz

Possible responses:

1. In less than 4 hours, an army of 100,000 Austrian and Russian soldiers was defeated by French troops. More than 30,000 soldiers and 20 generals were taken prisoner, and Third Coalition military equipment was seized.

2. They won glory, proved their superiority, demonstrated their courage and loyalty, and helped destroy the Third Coalition.

3. He was proud of their bravery and grateful to them for vanquishing the French Empire's foes. He also believed that their victory upheld the honor of his position as emperor.

Chapter 7, Section 1
LITERATURE SELECTION

A Tale of Two Cities

1. Charts will vary, but students should recognize that Dickens had contempt for the aristocracy and felt pity for the oppressed common people.

2. Diary entries will vary but should include specific details about the tragic accident from the point of view of either the Marquis, Defarge, or a witness in the crowd.

3. Informally assess students' sympathy cards. You may want to have the class create a bulletin board display of their work.

4. Before students begin, remind them to stay in character. Then informally assess students' performances and discussion.

Chapter 7, Section 1
HISTORYMAKERS

Marie Antoinette

Possible responses:

1. She was foreign and unused to French ways; she spent a lot of money on luxuries.

2. The attacks on the queen helped weaken the people's respect for authority. That probably helped contribute to the Revolution.

3. Answers will vary. Some students may suggest that the queen must have been strong to stand up to the crowd of market-women in 1791 and to speak forcefully in her own defense at her trial. Others may indicate that she was weak because she indulged herself in luxuries at the expense of public opinion.

Chapter 7, Section 2
HISTORYMAKERS

Maximilien Robespierre

Possible responses:

1. Many people recognized and admired his strong morality and his republican ideals.

2. He opposed the Hébertist economic controls and religious ideas. He disagreed with the Indulgents' view that the Terror could end.

3. Robespierre had accused others of threatening the republic and had them executed. The same thing happened to him.

Chapter 7, Section 2
CONNECTIONS ACROSS TIME AND CULTURES

Comparing Revolutions in America and France

Possible responses:

1. Writers such as Rousseau and Voltaire spread new ideas about power and authority in government. Enlightenment ideas about democracy and equality encouraged dissatisfaction among the Third Estate. Later, Jean Paul Marat wrote a radical newsletter.

2. Violent rebellion broke out in Paris and a mob stormed the Bastille. Peasants broke into nobles' manor houses and sometimes burned them. A mob of women broke into the palace at Versailles and killed three guards.

3. When a mob demanded that the royal family go to Paris, the king and queen were forced to declare their support for the Revolution and joined the National Assembly in wiping out the privileges of the Old Regime.

4. When the National Assembly stripped the church of its lands and its political independence, Catholic peasants were alarmed and stopped supporting revolutionary changes. The assembly's action created a division between the peasants and the bourgeoisie. The Legislative Assembly split into radicals, moderates, and conservatives.

5. In 1792, radicals in the Jacobin Club urged the National Convention to abolish the monarchy and establish a republic. The king was found guilty of treason and executed.

6. Moderate leaders of the National Convention turned on Robespierre and his Reign of Terror and drafted a new constitution that gave power to the middle class. The constitution called for a two-house legislature and an executive body called the Directory.

7. Answers will vary. Students should support their responses with details.

Chapter 7, Section 2
SCIENCE & TECHNOLOGY

Science Helps Create the Metric System

Possible responses:

1. The length of the meter was 1/10,000,000 of the distance from the North Pole to the equator along the meridian passing through Paris.

2. The adoption of a uniform system of measurement in all countries would help trade, manufacturing, and technological development. People would spend less time converting measurements from one system to another.

3. The distance from the North Pole to the equator is something that does not change and that people from any country can measure.

Chapter 7, Section 1
RETEACHING ACTIVITY

1. T
2. F; Most people fell into the Third Estate during the Old Regime.
3. F; Peasants were the largest group in the Third Estate.
4. T
5. T
6. clergy of Roman Catholic Church
7. scorned Enlightenment ideas
8. wealthy nobles
9. mixed feelings toward Enlightenment ideas

10. bourgeoisie, urban lower class, peasant farmers

11. agreed with Enlightenment ideas

Chapter 7, Section 2
RETEACHING ACTIVITY

1. G
2. A
3. K
4. C
5. I
6. B
7. M
8. D
9. J
10. F
11. H
12. E

Chapter 7, Section 3
RETEACHING ACTIVITY

1. In 1795, royalist rebels attacked the National Convention. Napoleon and his army fought off the attack, and Napoleon was called a hero.

2. The Directory lost control, and Napoleon's friends urged him to take action. He used troops to surround the national legislature and drive many of its members out. He then became one of three consuls and named himself first consul.

3. coup d'etat

4. The plebiscite was a vote of the people held to approve a new constitution. The constitution was approved, and as first consult, Napoleon got all the power.

5. He kept changes from the Revolution. He supported laws that would strengthen the central government. He set up a method of tax collection and established a national banking system. He fired corrupt officials and set up government-run public schools.

6. It created a new relationship between church and state. The government acknowledged the influence of the Church, but did not let the Church control state affairs.

7. It was a comprehensive system of laws that promoted order and authority over individual rights. It restricted freedom of speech and of the press, and restored slavery in the French colonies of the Caribbean.

8. Napoleon took the crown from the pope and crowned himself.

Chapter 7, Section 4
RETEACHING ACTIVITY

1. b
2. d
3. a
4. d
5. c
6. b
7. c
8. a

Chapter 7, Section 5
RETEACHING ACTIVITY

1. Congress of Vienna
2. Klemens von Metternich
3. balance of power
4. Austria
5. legitimacy
6. constitutional monarchies
7. Holy Alliance
8. Concert of Europe
9. Mexico
10. nationalism

Chapter 8, Section 1
GUIDED READING

A. Possible responses:

1. Whites used brutal methods to terrorize and dehumanize them, trying to keep them powerless; slaves outnumbered their masters.

2. Toussaint L'Ouverture became the leader of the revolution, but the French imprisoned him. Then General Dessalines took over the rebellion.

3. Motivated by Enlightenment ideals, creoles finally revolted against Spanish colonial rule when Napoleon made his brother, who was not Spanish, king of Spain.

4. Bolívar used surprise tactics to defeat the Spanish in Bogotá. San Martín, with the help of Bernardo O'Higgins, drove the Spanish out of Chile. The two leaders then met in Ecuador and San Martín left his army for Bolívar to command; this unified revolutionary force, under Bolívar, won independence for Peru.

5. With the *cry of Dolores,* Padre Miguel Hidalgo called upon peasants to rebel against Spanish rule.

6. Indians and mestizos began the revolution; later, creoles, fearing the loss of privileges under a new liberal regime in Spain, supported independence.

B. Possible response: At the top of Spanish colonial society were the *peninsulares,* who were Spanish-born; then came the creoles, Spaniards born in Latin America. Below them were people of mixed ancestry—first the mestizos (persons of mixed European and Indian ancestry) and then the mulattos (persons of mixed European and African ancestry). The Africans came next, and at the bottom stood the Indians.

Chapter 8, Section 2
GUIDED READING

A. Possible responses:

1. fueled nationalist movements and revolutions throughout Europe

2. A joint British, French, and Russian fleet defeated the Ottomans, and Greece gained its independence.

3. forced resignation of Metternich, triggered liberal uprisings throughout German states, but revolutionaries' failure to unite led to return of conservatism

4. led to riots that forced him to flee to Britain and led to replacement by Louis-Philippe, a supporter of liberal reforms

5. Republican government is set up, but factions turn to violence, resulting in bloody battles.

6. Under this strong ruler, prosperity, peace, and stability were restored.

7. Russia was defeated by combined forces of France, Great Britain, Sardinia, and the Ottomans; after the war, Alexander II began to modernize Russia.

8. Serfs were legally free but remained tied to the land through debts.

B. Possible responses:

Conservatives: protectors of the traditional order

Liberals: people who advocate more power for elected legislatures

Radicals: extremists who favor drastic change in government

Nationalism: loyalty to one's nation

Nation-state: country with an independent government that is made up of people who share a common culture

Chapter 8, Section 3
GUIDED READING

A. Possible responses:

1. Nationalist disputes led to the division of the empire into two states, Austria and Hungary. After World War I, the empire divided into separate nation-states.

2. Nationalist feeling of non-Russian peoples, fueled by the policy of Russification, weakened the empire, which fell as a result of war and revolution.

3. Conservative Turks, angered by the Ottoman policy of granting equal citizenship to nationalist groups, caused tensions that weakened and eventually broke up the empire.

4. as prime minister of Sardinian king, worked to expand Sardinian empire; through war, alliances, and help of nationalist rebels, succeeded; in the process, unified Italy

5. captured Sicily and united the southern areas of Italy he conquered with kingdom of Piedmont-Sardinia

6. pulled together northern and southern regions of Italy and took over the Papal states unifying Italy

7. This policy of tough politics allowed Bismarck to expand Prussia and achieve dominance over Germany.

8. Victory over Austria gave Prussia control over northern Germany.

9. Victory over France motivated southern Germany to accept Prussian leadership.

B. Possible response: Through a policy of "blood and iron," Otto von Bismarck eliminated Austria as a rival, provoked war with France, and achieved Prussian

dominance over northern and southern Germany to create the Second Reich, ruled by Kaiser William I.

Chapter 8, Section 4
GUIDED READING

A. Possible responses:

1. emphasized emotions over reason, untamed nature over natural laws and order; idealized past

2. Romantic writers glorified heroes and heroic actions, passionate love, revolutionary spirit, nature, and the supernatural.

3. Romantic painters focused on the beauty of nature, love, religion, and nationalism.

4. Romantic themes helped to popularize music and celebrate heroism and nationalism.

5. industrialization, interest in scientific method, invention of camera

6. The camera made possible startlingly real and objective images.

7. struggle for wealth and power, grim lives of working class

8. They hoped to bring about social reform and improve working and living conditions.

B. Possible response: Impressionism is an artistic style in which artists aim to capture their "impressions," or feelings, about a subject, rather than depict realistic details. Descriptions will vary but should note Monet's use of color and light and the mood he conveys.

Chapter 8
BUILDING VOCABULARY

A. Multiple Choice

1. a

2. c

3. a

4. b

5. a

6. c

B. Evaluating

1. T

2. F; The Junkers were strongly conservative members of Prussia's wealthy landowning class.

3. F; The drive for independence in Latin America was led by creoles, who were second on the social ladder, after the *peninsulares*.

4. T

C. Writing

Possible Answer

Romanticism was a movement that emphasized emotions and the imagination. Romantic painters focused on such themes as nature, love, religion, nationalism, violence, and exotic cultures to convey emotion. Realism was a movement that showed the world as it really was. It focused on the difficulties ordinary people faced.

Chapter 8, Section 1
SKILLBUILDER PRACTICE

Possible responses:

Hypothesis: The creoles were the driving force for independence from colonial rule in Latin America.

Fact 1: Creoles resented political power of *peninsulares* and felt oppressed; yes.

Fact 2: Creoles resented Spanish control over mining in Peru and Mexico; yes.

Fact 3: Creoles felt no loyalty to a French king placed on Spanish throne; yes.

Chapter 8, Section 3
GEOGRAPHY APPLICATION

Responses may vary on the inferential questions. Sample responses are given for those.

1. Germanic, Slavic, Romance, and Celtic; Germanic—north and Central Europe; Romance—Western and south-central Europe; Slavic—Eastern Europe; and Celtic—far northwestern Europe.

2. Germanic

3. Eastern Europe; Slavic; Great Russian, White Russian, Polish, Slovak, Ukrainian, Croatian, Serb, Slovene, and Bulgarian.

4. Romania does not border any other country speaking a Romance language.

5. Groups of people that speak a variety of languages might have a wide variety

of backgrounds, interests, and goals. It might be difficult to find common ground among a diverse group of people; Eastern Europe.

6. Language might give people an identity. It might help people come together and give them a common bond; Western Europe.

Chapter 8, Section 1
PRIMARY SOURCE

Proclamation of 1813

Possible responses:

1. to liberate Venezuela, destroy the Spaniards, protect South Americans, and reestablish the independent government of Venezuela

2. because the Spanish violated the political and civil rights of Venezuelans, broke treaties and agreements, and committed criminal acts against them

3. Some students may say that the policies—punishment for traitors and amnesty and reconciliation for those who atoned for their actions and cooperated in the cause of liberation—were imminently fair in light of what the Spanish did to the Venezuelans. Others may say that the policy of executing Spaniards who remained neutral was extremely harsh.

Chapter 8, Section 2
PRIMARY SOURCE

Letter to Thomas Moore

1. Informally assess the letters to make sure students use an appropriate tone and consistent point of view.

2. Students' time lines may include the following: narrowly escaped from the Turks, barely avoided a shipwreck, had an attack of either apoplexy or epilepsy, and underwent bleeding, a medical treatment in common use at the time, for his condition.

Chapter 8, Section 3
PRIMARY SOURCE

Proclamation of 1860

Possible responses:

1. money, arms, and volunteer soldiers

2. because it was their duty; because indifference in the past led to Italy's

domination by other nations; because Sicilians needed help to fight the armies of Austria, the Spanish Bourbons, and the Roman Catholic popes; because the liberation of Sicily was an important step in the unification of Italy

3. Some students may recognize specific propaganda techniques such as name-calling, loaded words, and bandwagon. Examples of propaganda include referring to the soldiers of the opposition as mercenaries, calling Italy the motherland, and calling Garibaldi's soldiers sons and brothers.

Chapter 8, Section 3
PRIMARY SOURCE

Nationalist Speech

1. Informally assess students' discussions. Guide them to understand that Bismarck, Bolívar, and Garibaldi all shared the dream of independence and unification and were willing to fight to achieve their dreams.

2. Informally assess how effectively students deliver this speech excerpt.

Chapter 8, Section 1
LITERATURE SELECTION

All Souls' Rising

Informally assess students' biographical sketches to make sure they are thoroughly researched and clearly written.

Chapter 8, Section 1
HISTORYMAKERS

Simón Bolívar

Possible responses:

1. He was a better military leader. His armies were successful, but he was unable to achieve his political goals of uniting many nations.

2. He believed that Europe's problem was that there were too many countries and they constantly fought each other. He hoped to form a large country linked to neighboring countries with a system of alliances.

3. Students may suggest that he was a partial success. He did much to achieve independence from Spain but was unable to achieve his political goals.

Chapter 8, Section 4
HISTORYMAKERS

Ludwig van Beethoven

Possible responses:

1. He suffered economically when young and possibly from rejected love. He also suffered deafness that did not allow him to hear his music.

2. His music was emotional and moving, and it broke with classical tradition. He exalted the hero, and he expressed such values as the fellowship of all people.

3. He pushed music in a new direction, changed the structure of musical forms, made instrumental music more significant than vocal music, and wrote the first "program music."

Chapter 8, Section 3
CONNECTIONS ACROSS TIME AND CULTURES

Possible responses:

1. many countries of origin; citizenship gained by many either by birth or through naturalization

2. 50 states and the District of Columbia; Puerto Rico, Guam, U.S. Virgin Islands, and other territories

3. representative democracy; federal republic

4. English as primary language of business, government, and education; Spanish as emerging second language; many other languages and dialects spoken

5. various, predominantly Christian

6. shared holidays, foods, dress, forms of entertainment, sports, literature, public education

7. modified form of capitalism and free enterprise system

8. currency, history, world view, political system

Chapter 8, Section 1
RETEACHING ACTIVITY

1. *Peninsulares* were at the top of society, followed by Creoles. These were followed by mestizos, mulattos, enslaved Africans, and Indians.

2. The American and French Revolutions and Enlightenment ideas stirred rebellion.

3. Bolívar won Venezuela's independence first, then joined San Martín in Ecuador and Peru. At the Battle of Ayacucho in Peru in 1824, Bolívar's troops defeated the Spanish. The Spanish colonies had won independence.

4. For 14 years, Brazil had been the center of the Portuguese empire. When the Portuguese government returned to Portugal and planned to make Brazil a colony again, creoles demanded independence. Dom Pedro agreed to remain and rule Brazil and officially declared Brazil independent.

5. c

6. a

7. f

8. d

9. e

10. b

Chapter 8, Section 2
RETEACHING ACTIVITY

1. Conservatives: property owners and nobility who wanted to maintain the traditional monarchies of Europe

2. Liberals: middle-class business leaders and merchants who wanted parliaments in which educated voters and landowners could vote

3. Radicals: wanted dramatic change in order to give power to the people as a whole

4. c

5. e

6. a

7. d

8. b

Chapter 8, Section 3
RETEACHING ACTIVITY

1. nationalism

2. Russification

3. Camillo di Cavour

4. Giuseppe Garibaldi

5. Junkers

6. Otto von Bismarck

7. realpolitik

8. Seven Weeks' War

9. Franco-Prussian War

10. kaiser

Chapter 8, Section 4
RETEACHING ACTIVITY

1. C

2. K

3. A

4. I

5. F

6. L

7. E

8. B

9. G

10. J

11. H

12. D